Leaving Home
COOKBOOK

and

SURVIVAL GUIDE

A Nutrition and Lifestyle Guide for
Eating Well and Staying Happy, Healthy and Above Broke
with Indispensable Tips on Time, Money and Dating

Seth Braun

Cookbook Resources, LLC
Highland Village, Texas

Leaving Home Cookbook and Survival Guide
Healthy, Fast and Cheap™

1st Printing - June 2008
2nd Printing - February 2009

International Standard Book No. 978-1-59769-025-6

Library of Congress No. 2008014961

Library of Congress Cataloging-in-Publication Data

    Braun, Seth.
     Leaving home cookbook and survival guide : healthy, fast and cheap : a nutrition and lifestyle guide for eating well and staying happy, healthy, and above broke with indispensable tips on time, money, and dating / Seth Braun. -- 1st ed.
       p. cm.
    Includes bibliographical references and index.
    ISBN 978-1-59769-025-6
    1. Cookery. 2. Nutrition. 3. Life skills. I. Title.
    TX652.B677 2008
    641.5--dc22

                          2008014961

Cover and Illustrations by Nancy Bohanan

Edited, Designed and Published in the United States of America
and Manufactured in China by
Cookbook Resources, LLC
541 Doubletree Drive
Highland Village, Texas 75077

Toll free 866-229-2665

www.cookbookresources.com

Bringing Family and Friends to the Table

About the Author

Seth Braun loves dark chocolate and dandelion greens, but not necessarily together. He is an outrageous optimist, living with his gorgeous wife and two lovely daughters in beautiful Boulder, Colorado. His passion for supporting other people's health and happiness inspired him to found Real Simple Nutrition, an organization dedicated to creating powerful personal health coaching and educational media. He is also the founder of High Energy Health Coaching and www.healthyfastandcheap.com.

Seth is a Certified Holistic Health Counselor with the American Association of Drugless Practitioners, a graduate of the Institute for Integrative Nutrition and a Certified 4 Gateways Coach.

Acknowledgments

Thank you, Ana Victoria, for all your support. Thanks to my girls, Paloma and Marisol, for the constant inspiration.

Sylvie Abecassis and Mark Duncan made this book happen. Thank you both for your amazing work. I feel blessed to have worked with you. I am so grateful.

Tabby Magas, thank you for the last minute tweaking; you are a star!

Evan and Jesse, you guys were the main reality check for this book. Thanks for reading all the conversations. I appreciate your feedback.

To Mark Belford for believing in the dream.

To my friends, family, clients and colleagues (I have so many!), please know that I am wishing each and every one of you energy, love and well-being. All of you! Yes, you!

To all my teachers, the Institute for Integrative Nutrition, Naropa University, Delta College, thanks for teaching.

This Book Is Dedicated to Learning.

What a Sweet Gift.

Preface

I have written and assembled information aimed at those of you who are on your own for the first time. I believe this will aid you in several aspects of your life. More than that, I also hope that you will find this information so valuable that you will keep using it well past your first years on your own.

Although the main thrust of my book is to provide essential tips, tricks and tools that you can use to help you eat well, this book is meant to be much more than that. There are five areas where I think what I simply call "good eating" can bring great pleasure and value to your life and these themes continue throughout the contents of this book.

1. **Maximum Enjoyment:** There is great pleasure in eating food that tastes and smells great, makes you feel good and looks beautiful.

2. **Nutrition:** The food you eat should contribute to a lifestyle that maintains your vitality, health and wellness.

3. **Convenience:** You are able to achieve these objectives within the context of a full and demanding schedule.

4. **Cost Effectiveness:** You are able to achieve these objectives within a set budget.

5. **Maximum Global Sustainability:** And you are able to achieve these objectives while contributing to a lasting abundance of nourishment for all people and fitting into the system of life on our planet.

How to Use This Book

First off, CONGRATULATIONS! There are a ton of cookbooks out there that are never opened, so thanks for opening this one! Now I want to get you to use it and with that in mind, everything in this book has been written and designed to be simple and easy to use. This is not a fancy recipe cookbook, but a blue jean cookbook you can wear any day.

You will get the most use of this book if you will try a few new things each week. Small steps taken over time add up to big results — that's just the way of life.

I suggest that you leave this book in an easy-to-access place in your kitchen; try one new recipe or variation each week; and read one of the life skill sections whenever the inspiration for better health, relationships, time management or budgeting strikes you.

It is a fact that most people have a dozen or so meals that they eat for breakfast, lunch and dinner. They usually rotate these and introduce some minor variations throughout most of their lives. With that in mind, I've designed several essential recipes for each meal of the day, with each recipe having a number of simple changes that produce the right balance of variety (for excitement) and familiarity (for ease of preparation).

 This icon indicates slow cooker recipes.

 This icon indicates especially recommended recipes.

Introduction

Thoughts of the first-time apartment dweller or a student diet conjure up images of ramen noodles, pizza, beer, cereal and power bars. Although this is how it is for many people, it is not how I like to eat. Even as a student I like to eat quality food that leaves me feeling strong and clear-headed. Don't get me wrong, I like pizza, but not for breakfast, lunch and dinner seven days a week!

As I write this, I am a student at the Institute for Integrative Nutrition, New York City, but the majority of the material in this "food guide" was generated while I was a performing arts major at a small liberal arts school, Naropa University, in Boulder, Colorado.

Why do I think this cookbook will work for you? I know it can because I have eaten well for less than $200 a month while living in Boulder, Colorado; Berkeley, California; and in Cevennes in southern France. I love food and I've cooked in fancy restaurants and on propane burners at rustic wilderness retreats. I have learned that Healthy, Fast and Cheap™ eating is more about principles and skills than it is about recipes.

This book is for the person who likes life rich and meaningful. How about you? What experiences do you have that make you an amazing cook? Maybe you have a couple of killer recipes from your family or maybe you know how to make a bad ass sandwich from your experience working in a deli. Whatever your background, I am going to help you take what you already know and tweak it so that you can consistently prepare a range of Healthy, Fast and Cheap™ meals that you will love.

Thanks for reading *Leaving Home Cookbook and Survival Guide*. I am so glad that you are interested in increasing your health and happiness.

—*Seth Braun*

Contents

Contents

Life Skills One: Budget

There is nothing complicated about setting up a budget. As a student I found it easy to establish and follow a budget because most of the variables in my life were set. You don't need any special books, forms or calculators. All you need is a piece of paper with two columns.

Income	Expenses
Income is simple. It's the money you receive each month: • Job • Loans • Scholarships or grants • Family or other support • A combination of the above	Expenses are a little more complex. It's the money that goes out: • Tuition and books • Food • Rent and utilities • Phone • Car/transportation • Health care/insurance • Personal care (hair cuts, massage etc.) • Recreation • Clothes • Miscellaneous

With expenses, you control just about everything except the essentials, more or less. Let's take a look at an example.

In the example on the next page, we are assuming that your tuition is paid for with Stafford loans and scholarships. The remaining loan amount is then divided by four months — let's say it is for September, October, November and December.

Income	$ per Month	Expenses	$ per Month
Loans (3000 ÷ 4 months =)	750	Rent and utilities	
Part-time job*	520	Food	
Other support	500	Phone	
		Car	
		Health care	
		Recreation	
		Personal care	
		Clothes	
Total Income	**$1770**	**Total Expenses**	

*The average entry-level college work-study makes $8/hr. I estimated this at 15 hours per week x 4.33 weeks in a month. However, there will be tax deductions.

This is a typical student budget: it's tight. You really don't have a ton of flex, but hey, relax because now you know what you can afford and when! With a budget in place, you don't have to stress when going out with a group of friends for food and drink to celebrate. You can check out what you have spent on food up to that point and decide whether you can afford that expensive entree.

The best part of having a good budget is that you know how much you can spend on food and what is realistic for you. I have found that when students budget they give themselves permission to buy higher quality food in the store and are less likely to eat out. This leads to significant savings.

Life Skills Two: Time Management

The only way that you are going to eat well is if you are well organized. One of the keys to being organized is time management. Here is a simple way for you to improve the quality of your time.

Write down your schedule for a typical week. Go ahead, it won't take long.

Morning Schedule							
Hours	Monday	Tuesday	Wednesday	Thursday	Friday	Saturday	Sunday
6 - 7							
7 - 8							
8 - 9							
9 - 10							
10 - 11							
11 - 12							
Afternoon and Evening Schedule							
Hours	Monday	Tuesday	Wednesday	Thursday	Friday	Saturday	Sunday
12 - 1							
1 - 2							
2 - 3							
3 - 4							
4 - 5							
5 - 6							
6 - 7							
7 - 8							
8 - 9							
9 - 10							
10 - 11							

After you write out your classes, work, practices, errand time, etc., write down when you are going to shop, when you will cook and when you will get snacks and lunches together.

Go ahead and schedule other important activities as well, including time with friends and time to unwind and relax. What the heck, schedule time to sleep, too!

Do this for anything that is important to you and that you want to include in your life. Don't wait for life to happen to you. Make sure you schedule the things that are important!

Life Skills Three: Housemates and the Kitchen

Everyone I have ever met that has shared a kitchen with housemates has, at some point, experienced the mystery dishes dilemma. You know, a bowl appears in the sink and no one knows where it came from. In fact, the kitchen seems to be the place where housemate conflicts play out the most. I don't know why, but I do know this is the way it is for most students and young adults.

Here are some guidelines for kitchen conflicts.

- Have an agreed on set of ground rules about the kitchen.

- Seek first to understand, then to be understood. (This means you actually have to listen to your housemates vent for a couple minutes first, then stop, consider and reflect on what you heard.)

- Set a time each week where all housemates sit down together and discuss what your expectations are in the house. This will decrease the amount of conflict by proactively setting up systems of success.

- And finally, agree that each of you will do a few more dishes than you think you need to do each week. This is like a golden secret that, if followed, will make your kitchen groove more open and functional.

Tools for Kitchen Setup

Appliances, utensils, pots, pans, knives and more.

You should make every attempt to buy the best quality tools for your kitchen. I have listed the bare essentials, the almost essentials and the must-haves for food enthusiasts like me. Remember, you may not need to buy all these yourself. Ask a couple of people in your family to donate one really good piece of kitchen equipment to your new kitchen, drop hints to relatives and look for deals at yard sales and thrift stores.

Bare Essentials

1. You'll need a few pots and pans. Both a large and a small pot, ideally made of stainless steel, will prove invaluable. In addition you'll want to have a large and small pan made from cast iron (my first choice) or hard-anodized aluminum with a top quality non-stick surface.

2. At least two good quality knives: one chef's knife and one paring knife. It is also a good idea to get a knife sharpener.

3. One large and one small cutting board.

4. A food processor/blender. The Cuisinart Mini Prep® Processor is a good choice because it gets good reviews and it is small and powerful.

5. Two stainless steel bowls, one large and one small.

6. Kitchen timer.

7. A large metal spoon, a large wooden spoon, a large wooden spatula (for flipping hot fried things) and a medium rubber spatula (for wiping, smearing and cleaning out).

8. Can opener.

9. A sponge with a soap reservoir handle. (This makes clean up so much easier!)

10. A grain strainer. (A fine weave wire mesh strainer.)

11. Basic set of measuring cups and measuring spoons

You don't want to make this too complicated. Just get one big and one small of each of most of the items on the "essentials" list. You can figure out which largest and smallest sizes best suit your needs.

Almost Essentials

Next we have the "almost essential" or the "I-live-in-a-dorm-room-studio-tree-house with-an-extension-cord" list:

1. Electric kettle. Plug it in and it boils water faster than you can say, "Wow, this thing boils water pretty fast."

2. Slow cooker. The point here is you throw in some food in the morning and it cooks all day, even when you're away. It is ready for you when you get home. How great is that?

3. George Foreman® Grill. If you don't have a stove or if you just want to make your life easier, this little countertop accessory will make you smile.

4. Toaster oven. This is almost an essential item, especially if you do not have a full oven. It is helpful to get a hanging model to maximize kitchen space.

5. I never use a hot plate. If you get one then you still need to have the basics from above.

Non-Essentials

Finally, here are the "food lover's must-have items":

1. Tongs. Get the kind with the spring-loaded hinges. You'll use these for everything that requires grabbing — hot or cold.

2. Wire whisk. You really can't make an omelet without one of these. A fork just won't cut it!

3. A medium bowl, pot and pan to accompany your other sizes.

4. A large stainless steel colander.

5. Kitchen shears. You should get a pair of big, heavy-duty scissors for your kitchen to cut all sorts of stuff including herbs, meats, veggies and even food wrappers.

Because you are going to buy quality items, you can count on these being around long after you move on. (Unless you are a career student!) The cast iron, with care, will be around for your grandkids!

Tupperware

There are many brands of food storage containers on the market. To me, Tupperware® is to containers what Kleenex® is to tissue. The brand name has become synonymous with the product and that's good marketing! However, there are now many other options available and you should explore these. Part of eating Healthy, Fast and Cheap™ is having a great system for food transportation — so you'll need a good supply of affordable, flexible and airtight containers. You will benefit from having the following containers in your kitchen.

- Two sandwich-sized containers. (For sandwiches, of course, but these are just the right size for bringing snacks in a backpack.)

- Two medium-sized containers for storing leftovers.

- One small container for miscellaneous storage (e.g., olives, condiments, etc.).

I had a housemate that made big salads in the spring and summer, stored them in medium-sized containers and brought dressing in a small jar. So get creative and PREPARED to eat well by having the right containers for transporting your food before your day gets hectic. Consider getting a high quality water bottle as well. Look for one that is medical grade plastic. (Note: you will still need to regularly wash and sanitize your water bottle!)

Keep the Pantry Stocked

You want to have foods on hand (that are Healthy, Fast and Cheap™) and ready at all times. Here are some staple foods to keep in your kitchen.

- Peanut butter — natural, of course
- Food for Life Ezekiel 4:9® sprouted grain or other sprouted grain breads
- Soup stock or bouillon cubes
- Thai noodle packets
- Nuts: almonds, cashews, Brazil, hazelnuts, etc.
- Seeds: pumpkin, sunflower, etc.

- Vegetables: especially onions, sweet potatoes, carrots (these store well) and make sure you have a ready supply of frozen vegetable mixes.

- Fruits: especially apples (these store very well), frozen berries and other frozen fruits.

- Eggs

- Yogurt

Life Skills Four: Food and Dating

You've heard it said, the path to a man's heart is through his stomach. Similarly, there is probably no better way to impress a lady than to prepare a tasty, healthy dinner and serve it by candlelight.

When you talk about relationships, we have to talk food. We eat every day and therefore food is our most consistent and intimate relationship. After all, it is a living thing that we prepare and then put inside our bodies. Talk about intimate!

How to Impress Your Date

To Impress a Woman

I bet there is nothing more satisfying than a big slice of pizza, a thick steak or a fast juicy burger. Well, my wife loves these things too, but when we were both students at Naropa University that was not the meal that most impressed her. The meal you make for your date is going to say a lot about you. In fact, the what, how and way you eat always tells a lot about your personality. Keep that in mind.

You want to show your intelligence, your taste and your refined sensibilities. Here is a meal that is Healthy, Fast and Cheap™, tastes great and will totally impress!

Citrus Salmon with Quinoa and Mixed Greens

1½ cups quinoa
1 tablespoon olive oil
1 (½ pound) salmon filet
2 lemons, thinly sliced
8 - 10 leaves red leaf lettuce and romaine
Olive oil
Lemon, cut in wedges
½ cup pitted black olives
Oregano

▶ The morning of the dinner, begin by soaking quinoa in water. One hour before your date arrives, strain the grain and place it in a pot with ¾ inches water (up to the first joint of your index finger). Add a generous dash of salt and olive oil. Bring water to a boil, then reduce to a simmer for 20 minutes. Turn off heat, fluff the grain and let stand on the stove top.

▶ Preheat oven to 350°.

▶ Slice the salmon into 4 strips with a sharp serrated knife. Place it in a baking dish and slightly separate the slices so they lean against each other like dominoes. Sprinkle with a touch of salt and a few generous dashes of pepper and cover the surface of the fish completely with thin slices of lemon.

▶ Bake for 5 to 8 minutes. (The exact time will depend on the thickness of the fish.) When the flesh is flaky throughout, the fish is done.

▶ The salad is simple. Chop red leaf lettuce and romaine into thin strips. Place into a bowl and toss. Cover with a light drizzle of olive oil and a few bursts of lemon juice, a dash of salt, black pepper and oregano. Garnish with black olives and serve with lemon wedges.

TIP: *Quinoa (KEEN wah) is a super grain that can be substituted for rice. It has more protein than any other grain and contains vital nutrients and amino acids.*

Here's the timing before the date with dinner at 6:30.

Morning	Put quinoa in bowl and cover with water to soak.
4:45 - 5:30 pm	Clean yourself and your place. Set the table. Put on an old T-shirt and keep the nice shirt in your room or put on an apron.
5:30 - 5:45 pm	Prepare the salad.
5:45 - 5:50 pm	Drain, measure and bring the quinoa to a boil.
5:50 - 5:55 pm	While quinoa heats, start slicing lemons. (The thinner the slices the better.)
5:55 pm	Reduce quinoa to a simmer.
5:55 - 6:05 pm	Turn oven to 350° and being preparing the salmon.
6:05 pm	Place salmon in the oven.
6:15 pm	Turn off quinoa, fluff and let stand covered on the stove.
6:20 pm	Remove the salmon and test for flakiness.
6:20 - 6:25 pm	Clean up the kitchen as much as you can in 5 minutes. Wash your hands and put on a nice shirt. Place the food on the table with serving utensils, then light some candles and answer the door. Do not ask your date to help clean up when you have finished dinner.

Enjoy the rest of your evening!

Cooking for a Guy

Typically, guys like a big, meaty meal that satisfies completely. I have cooked for guys on wilderness retreats in the Rocky Mountains and can testify that if a man is hungry, anything you put in front of him will be great! However, you are aiming for amazing. You want a meal to have a powerful effect, but you don't want the guy to think you cook like his mother. You want to make a meal that is vibrant, hands-on and satisfying. Meat will usually be the main component of the meal, unless your guest is a vegetarian and you should be sure you know about this in advance. Serving meat to your vegetarian guest would be a buzz kill! All this said, here is the meal I would prepare.

Steak Fajitas

The trick is to prepare this meal without spending too much money or taking too much time. Go to the butcher and purchase free-range beef or buffalo meat thinly sliced. This way you can get a less expensive cut of meat, marinate it and ensure that it is tender when it's served.

⅔ pound free-range, organic beef or buffalo, cut into thin strips

Marinade:

1 cup pineapple juice
1 teaspoon pepper
Dash of vinegar or lemon juice

▶ Mix marinade ingredients in the morning and pour over meat. (Put meat in a large resealable bag. It will make it easy to move meat around.)

So you have your steak thin sliced by the guy at the meat shop and it is marinating for at least 6 hours. (Put it in the marinade in the morning.) Now you just need the rest of the goods.

1 cup rice
1 (15 ounce) can black beans
Canola oil
1 each, red, yellow and green bell peppers, seeded, sliced
1 medium red onion, chopped
1 medium zucchini, sliced like french fries
1 avocado
1 large tomato or 2 roma tomatoes, chopped, drained
Salsa
6 flour tortillas

▶ Prepare rice according to package directions. Empty beans into pot and heat on burner.

▶ Preheat large skillet with a little oil, brown meat on all sides over high heat and reduce heat to simmer.

▶ Push meat to one side and place all fresh vegetables except avocado and tomatoes in skillet. (Add oil if necessary.) Season with a little salt and pepper.

continued next page

▶ Cover and cook on low heat until veggies are tender. Peel and slice avocado.

▶ Serve hot with avocado slices, tomatoes, rice, beans, salsa and tortillas.

It's All in the Timing

For a 6:30 dinner, you'll want to start the beans at 5 pm (unless you used canned), the rice at 5:30, the steak at 6:00, the veggies at 6:10 and the tortillas at 6:15.

You'll want to have the food hot and time to change, but unlike the guy's meal to impress a woman, you should ask for help setting the table and with cleaning up the kitchen. Guys like stuff to do. So put your man to work and tell him you are going to change clothes. Guys love that, too. This will give you time to take a break from cooking and put on something that makes you feel good. Then come back to a set table and enjoy dinner!

Candles, salad and music are all options, but college guys don't seem to notice the nuances as much. They will probably be way into putting together their meal. That is the beauty of fajitas, guys get to build their food then eat it. He might want to put everything in a tortilla and roll it up. He might want beans and rice on the side. Whatever is clever.

Life Skills Five: Total Health

Because I included the word healthy in Healthy, Fast and Cheap™, I have to at least mention the following essential elements of a healthy lifestyle.

Exercise

Nobody lives well without exercise and an exercise program needs to hit these three points.

1. Oxygenate the body (aerobic exercise)

2. Work major muscle groups (weight bearing or isometric exercise)

3. Harmonize the mind and body (yoga, chi kung, dance and stretching)

Meaning

To be living in the question of: "Why am I here?" often means having daily spiritual practice or contemplative time. Walks in the woods, meditation and prayer offer this nourishment. Volunteering, studying what you love, and doing work that inspires you are each ways of bringing meaning into your life. Here are some ways to cultivate meaning.

1. Keep a journal of your thoughts and feelings.

2. Have a time to meditate.

3. Have a time to pray.

4. Have time to contemplate the big questions in life.

5. Involve yourself in a religious community.

6. Spend time in nature.

Goals

One way many people create meaning in their lives is by setting goals. Here are a few simple ways to help you set your goals.

1. Focus on your most compelling dreams for your life.

2. Divide these into several large, but well-defined goals.

3. Break these into small steps.

4. Set goals for each area of your life:

   a. Health

      - exercise

      - dietary goals

   b. Career

      - income

      - type of work

      - location

c. Education

- grades

- extra-curricular activities

- social life

- personal enrichment (What do you want to get from your classes or work?)

   d. Personal development (Make yourself a better person.)

Another way people organize their growth and development is through identifying roles: student, friend, employee, athlete, partner, father, mother, artists, writer, etc. Establish your objectives for those roles:

Student: 3.75 GPA or better

Friend: Spend Saturday evenings with friends

Athlete: 2 hours each day to improve the jump shot

Nutrition

Health is balance. At my school, the Institute for Integrative Nutrition, we break it down as I have shown below.

1. Primary Food

   a. career

   b. exercise

   c. spirituality

   d. relationships

2. Secondary Food

   a. Macronutrients

- carbohydrates

- protein

- fat

b. Micronutrients

- vitamins
- minerals
- essential fatty acids
- essential amino acids
- phytochemicals
- enzymes

For more information on total health, check out my Web site links:

www.highenergyhealthcounselor.com

www.healthyfastandcheap.com

Nutrition Guidelines

There are enough dietary theories around to get us thoroughly confused. The publishing world is set up to market, "the next new discovery in health". But really, most of the wisdom in nutrition has been around for thousands of years. With full realization of the need for specific applications, some general recommendations for you to consider are given below.

Guiding Principles for Eating Well and Staying Healthy

- Eat unprocessed food.
- Use common sense.
- Eat foods close to their natural state.
- Local and organic never hurt anyone.
- Variety is nourishing; monotony is stagnant.
- Live between extremes. Eat well most of the time and enjoy life's bounty.
- Recognize and change food choices that are habitual.
- Find other ways to meet emotional needs than eating for comfort.

- Reduce the amount of sugar and refined carbohydrates and replace them with sweet vegetables like sweet potatoes, yams, squash, carrots and beets or with fresh, frozen or dried fruits.

- Eat more whole grains.

- Eat a lot of veggies. I can't think of any major dietary theory that says don't eat kale. Eat a bunch of vegetables and you can't go wrong.

- Remember to get the highest quality animal products you can.

- Eat some raw and cultured/fermented foods everyday. This includes raw fruits and vegetables, yogurt, kefir, kombucha, sauerkraut, lacto-fermented pickles, miso, and more.

Going back to the total health overview, if you get your exercise, relationships, spirituality and school/career goals in line, it is much easier to eat well. Likewise, eating well tends to make all the other stuff work better, too!

The Three Worst Ingredients: The Stuff You Want to Avoid

Okay, here is the rub. A good healthy diet is really about eating really, really well about 52% of the time, 30% of the time you eat pretty well, and about 10% of the time you "pig out" and eat whatever you want. Yeah, I know, that leaves 8%. That is buffer.

That said, there are some ingredients you would do well to avoid altogether, which is really pretty easy since you can get the same good stuff with better ingredients.

Here they are:

1. **Hydrogenated and partially hydrogenated oil**, (also known as interesterified oil) was called, "the worst food you can eat" by Dr. Walter Willet, based on his research in the largest controlled health study in the Western World, the Harvard-based Nurses' Health Study.

2. **High fructose corn syrup** is the cheapest ingredient in the American food supply; and therefore, it is in everything. This sugar has been clearly linked to the progressive increase in degenerative diseases such as type 2 diabetes, heart disease and obesity.

3. **Artificial and chemicalized foods.** Artificial colors, flavors and preservatives plus fake food have fats that are not fat, sugar that is not sugar and other stuff that has been synthesized in a lab that has not been questioned in terms of long term effects on the human physiology. Do you want to be part of the experiment? Not me. The only smart way is natural, real food.

The Vegetarian v. Non-Vegetarian Debate

This is a heated debate that often finds interest among college students. Below are some of my basic thoughts on the issue.

Chicken

It is very important to buy free-range chickens that live outdoors. The commercial chicken lives in a warehouse its entire life, being force-fed with inclusion of antibiotics to keep it from getting sick as it lives in the midst of its own waste. I am sorry that I have to include this in a cookbook, but you have got to make the distinction between levels of quality when you choose animal products. I can't stress that enough.

Eggs

Commercial eggs are laid by chickens that live in warehouses. They live five to a cage and are stacked cage upon cage. They can't move out of the tiny space that encloses them together, they are constantly pecking at each other and they live most of their lives in total darkness. The smell is overwhelming. Their beaks are clipped as young chicks so they do not peck each other to death and they are constantly fed antibiotics to keep them from dying. The eggs produced by these chickens are nutritionally devoid of micronutrients and the macronutrients are of lower quality.

Beef

It is very important to buy free-range organic meat whenever possible. Cows evolved to eat grass and they have ruminant stomachs. They break down grass and this in turn creates nutritious meat. The celebration of grain-fed meat has to do with the increased fat in the meat, but cows are not designed to eat grains such as corn and soybean meal. It causes development of severe digestive problems, which in turn leads to further health problems. Cows have become the dumping ground for the waste arising from the food industry. Bakery waste, citrus peel cake and other food industry waste products are fed back to cows. Additionally, factory farming is inhumane and the animals are treated without integrity.

Meat and Health

Generally, most Americans could reduce the portion sizes of animal products considerably and without question, the quality of animal products could be improved for most Americans. The right amount of animal products and protein for you is dependent on your ancestral diet, your stress level, your activity/exercise level and your body type. Contrary to some vegan health advocates, some people need to eat meat/animal foods to maintain good health. For some vegetarians, a little yogurt or butter on occasion is all they need to stay in balance; for others, a heavier diet is required.

Animal Foods and Spirituality

Not eating meat does not make you more spiritual. We are all spiritual beings having a human experience and we cannot be "not spiritual." After extensively studying the commercial meat and dairy industry, I would agree that the treatment of animals in factory farms is unethical, inhumane and unnecessary. This view is my own and is based on my own conscience of what is right and wrong. You may have come to a different conclusion.

Super Foods for the College Dorm or Apartment

This special report was written for two former students of mine that are now in their first year at college. They both have cafeteria dining plans at their schools: one plan is great, the other terrible. The student with the lousy cafeteria food plan really needs to have some support in getting good nutrition. The student with the better quality food plan will benefit from the extra boost that these super foods offer.

Why Super Foods?

It goes without saying that nutrition is important for physical, mental and emotional health. But what seems obvious to us appears to be neglected in mainstream commerce. Vitamins and supplements sell all over the place, but some suppliers are better than others.

Super foods allow humans to get the power of vitamins and supplements in the ultimate bio-available package. Why take a pill to get what nature made perfectly in a plant? Super foods are reliable ways to get nutrient-dense foods. We need nutrient-dense foods because our bodies thrive on them. Most industrialized modern societies have farming practices that lead to a food surplus that is heavy in calories but short on nutrients. Super foods help bring balance.

What Are Super Foods?

Super foods are, well, super! Super nutrient-dense, super detoxifying, super energetically compatible with the human body, super balancing, stimulating or soothing as needed. These foods are potent!

Let's take kelp as an example. Kelp is rich in iodine, calcium, iron, vitamins B1, B2 and B12. It has the ability to help remove toxins and this is very important in modern life. Kelp, like all sea vegetables is mineral dense. This is important because we live in a mineral-deficient culture; but wait, the ocean contains all known minerals on the planet and eating sea vegetables helps you get everything!

Here are eight super foods that I believe we should consume regularly. (Each is available in an easy to eat form.)

1. **Algae,** spirulina, chlorella and blue-green forms of algae are available in powdered forms or as capsules. Experiment with which works well for you, but make sure to get the highest quality available. Although there is some debate over the benefits of algae, I believe it to be a very valuable food that detoxifies and alkalinizes the body. Algae is rich in chlorophyll and may be useful in reducing inflammation, cleansing the blood and in bringing an acid/alkaline balance to the body. I am unsure why the mainstream medical community has not researched algae more completely. I have read many reports that try to debunk its value but none of them get below the surface. Again, I encourage you to get the best quality available, begin with small quantities and research this for yourself.

2. **Bee pollen** contains twice the antioxidant level of blueberries and triple the polyphenol content of cranberries (www.ccpollen. com). I recommend that you eat one small pearl of pollen to begin with (to test for allergic reaction) and increase the amount slowly over time. If you have any known allergies to pollen then you must take extra precautions when you use this super food. It has a pleasant taste, can be added to cereal or you can eat it plain. Bees collect millions of tiny pollen spores to build one bee pollen pellet and this is an incredible task. One teaspoon of pollen contains over 2.5 billion grains of pollen! Anecdotally, I have seen clients report significant improvement in energy and stamina through the use of bee pollen.

3. **Cacao** is the raw form of chocolate. It is high in minerals and contains over 400 beneficial chemical compounds. Although it is bitter to the taste, it is not unpalatable. I suggest that it is best when used in smoothies or mixed with other foods, but for simple medicinal use it can be eaten 1 tablespoon at a time. Cacao is a better choice than coffee for days when you are feeling the need for stimulants. It is rich in magnesium, the number one mineral deficiency for most Americans. In addition, cacao also contains selenium, the number one trace mineral deficiency for most Americans. However, cacao cannot be understood completely from a compartmentalized view and there is nothing like it on the entire planet. Its physiological effects are quite unique so I suggest you experiment for yourself. Try using raw cacao nibs — pieces of peeled low fermented cacao beans — in smoothies.

4. **Sardines** come in a can and you can eat them anywhere. They are rich in omega-3 fatty acids, which are deficient in most Americans' diets and they are good for the brain. Sardines are also rich in calcium and they are an excellent source of protein. Sardines or Kipper Snacks for that matter are one of the best marine animal foods to eat. The problem with most fish is heavy metal accumulation. You avoid this problem with sardines because they don't live that long and they are not predators; therefore, they have less chance to build up toxins. Sardines are a great source of vitamin D available in a form that is efficient for use.

5. **Kombucha** is a probiotic beverage that will aid in maintaining healthy digestion and elimination. It is my preferred stimulant because it is made with green tea. The most widely distributed brand is GT's but online sources abound. Kombucha can be brewed simply in a dorm room, but it does take time and attention. Two acids present in kombucha, gluconic and glucoronic acid, may be responsible for its reputation as a detoxifier. It is high in many vitamins and helps to alkalinize the body.

6. **Pumpkin seeds** are little powerhouses that are especially valuable for males because they contain prostate protecting compounds. They are nutritionally dense with minerals, protein and essential fatty acids. Pick fresh green looking seeds. Pumpkin seeds are an easy addition to daily snacks. "Snack on a quarter-cup of pumpkin seeds and you will get 46.1% of the daily value for magnesium, 28.7% of the DV for iron, 52.0% of the DV for manganese, 240.0% of the DV for copper, 16.9% of the DV for protein, 19.7% of the DV for monounsaturated fat and 17.1% of the DV for zinc" (from www.mercola.com/forms/trail_mix.htm).

7. **Acerola powder** is made from the acerola cherry. Ounce for ounce, acerola contains over 30 times the vitamin C content of oranges. You can buy acerola as a powder and mix it with water. It tastes fine! Acerola is good for boosting the immune system, especially when you are under high stress. Acerola is also rich in magnesium, pantothenic acid, potassium and vitamin A. Acerola can be a great help during finals week or any time you are under increased stress.

8. **Goji berries** are little nuggets of goodness! A traditional food of China, Mongolia, Tibet and the Himalayas, they are one of the most nutrient-dense foods on the planet. The antioxidant level of goji berries is about 10 times that of blueberries (using the ORAC* scale) and that's incredibly high. You can get 170% of your daily vitamin A requirements from just 1 ounce. The use of goji berries has been documented in Chinese medicine for thousands of years.

*The ORAC (Oxygen Radical Absorption Capacity) refers to the antioxidant content in foods.

These are relatively inexpensive and readily available super foods. For a complete list of super foods, request the special report titled, "A Complete List of Super Foods" from Real Simple Nutrition (seth@highenergyhealthcounselor.com).

Avoiding Afternoon Fatigue

Come 3:00 pm do you begin to get drowsy, feel fatigued and struggle to make it to the evening? Then, when nighttime comes, do you feel a need for a pick-me-up again? This is very common, but certainly not how you want to live your life. This is such a common occurrence that some companies have begun to aggressively push quick-fix solutions. I recently saw an advertisement for a new version of several classic candy bars that were offered as a solution to the afternoon slump. To my mind this is more likely to cause the slump than offer a solution! How did we get into this situation and what is going on?

There are three primary reasons for 3:00 pm slump and they are simple to address. First let me just say that the two biggest culprits for afternoon fatigue are also the most commonly used treatments, but unfortunately, this just makes things worse in the long run. Let's look at the situation in more detail.

Reason One: Blood Sugar Swings

There are currently 20 million Americans with type 2 diabetes and there are an estimated 40 million more with prediabetes or impaired glucose tolerance. Millions more people are dealing with hypoglycemia, insulin resistance or metabolic syndrome (syndrome X). What do these have to do with feeling sleepy at 3:00 pm? The answer is that an amazing number of Americans are losing the healthy function of insulin in the body. Insulin is the hormone that lets glucose into cells for fuel. It is also a growth hormone and is involved in a multitude of other physical operations.

When you eat refined carbs, e.g., sugar, your body produces a surge in insulin to match the surge of glucose that has just entered your bloodstream. This surge does two things: first, the glucose is put into the cells for use and second, the excess glucose that cannot be used is stored as fat in the body. The rapid conversion of glucose into fat leaves the body needing more fuel immediately. This is the classic sugar roller coaster: you can eat a ton of calorie-dense food and be hungry in 20 minutes. After years of this, the body's ability to manage blood sugar and insulin becomes impaired. This is the first reason that you become tired at 3:00 pm: your insulin production needs to be stabilized.

Reason Two: Overuse of Stimulants

Caffeine is routinely used around the world. There is nothing wrong with caffeine, but when you come to depend on it to get through the day, you should be a little concerned.

Caffeine works, in part, to stimulate the adrenal glands. I would wager that the majority of working professionals in America have taxed adrenal glands and this leads to difficulty in waking in the morning, grogginess during parts of the day, loss of appetite around breakfast time and is often accompanied by intense sleepiness around 7:00 to 9:00 am and around 3:00 pm. Many have a strong second wind around 10:30 pm. Reducing caffeine is the first step in reversing the cycle of adrenal response.

Reason Three: Reduction of Physical Heartiness

By this I mean that one or more body systems is having a difficult time; for example, problems with digestion and assimilation. If your digestion is impaired, then your body needs much more energy to assimilate food and this can lead to drowsiness.

Another common source of fatigue is a suppressed immune system. This can stem from constant stress from internal and external pressures, for example, a lack of adequate rest or from the need for better food or exercise.

Sometimes, accumulated toxins can cause the body to function at less than optimal energy. Over-acidity, excess toxins from the stress response, radiation from common electronics, common chemicals, pesticide residues and other toxins can accumulate in specific areas of the body and this can lead to compromised function all over the body. The outcome can be fatigue.

What is the solution?

The great news is the body is a healing machine. It is quite miraculous and with a little support you can be back to a high-energy lifestyle. The first two steps are simple in principle, but not easy in practice. Replacing coffee, colas, sugar and other refined carbohydrates and stimulants with whole, natural foods will significantly improve your health.

The second step is more difficult and you could benefit from the support of an expert. You need to identify where you may be experiencing impaired function and create a plan to bring your body's natural intelligence and vigor back up to speed.

Options When Eating Out

It is great to make food at home to take to class or work, but sometimes you just can't make it happen. I understand. Here are some tips on food options. These suggestions will help guide you to choices that will really keep your energy up and keep you going.

Your First Choice: The Salad Bar

- Use olive oil and vinegar as a dressing when available, but don't be afraid of the full fat dressings if you love them (blue cheese, ranch).

- Avoid the sweet dressings because they contain too much sugar.

- Load up on your favorite veggies whether they are raw, cooked, steamed, roasted or pickled.

- Choose lean meats, eggs, beans, nuts and seeds.

- Fresh, real and simple are key words for the salad bar.

- Iceberg lettuce is devoid of any nutritional value. If you love it, make sure you include other veggies.

- Most salad bars now contain these recommended selections: romaine lettuce, tuna, eggs, peas, chick-peas, sunflower seeds, onions, peppers, tomatoes, olives, olive oil and vinegar.

Other Options When Eating Out

- Keep it fresh, real and simple!
- Always load up on veggies. Raw, steamed, boiled, roasted, braised or stir-fried. (Potatoes do not count as vegetables.)
- Cut out the soda.
- Eat what you love.
- Asian options often have a bunch of vegetables and lean meat.
- Whole grain is a better choice.
- Go for the rice and beans option at Mexican restaurants.
- Burrito places can offer a bunch of fresh and grilled vegetables on whatever you order.
- Noodle shops often offer whole grain noodles with a plate of vegetables and lean meat.
- Smoothie and juice joints offer a fabulous mix of nutrient dense foods, but watch out for the over-sugared smoothies. These can lead to a crash.

Potatoes do not count as vegetables!

The USDA states that Americans are increasing their vegetable consumption, but that is really stretching the truth! This is only true because french fries and potato chips are included as vegetables in their surveys.

The Motivation to Eat Healthy

I would never tell someone to eat something just because an expert says so. I want to encourage you to eat well because you want to! You want to feel vibrant. You want to think clearly. You want to have energy to pursue your passions, your interests and all aspects of your life! The highest form of discipline in eating is not will power; it's paying attention to how you respond to what you eat. How will you feel the next time you eat that food? If you eat a pastry in the morning for breakfast, how do you feel afterwards? How about in a half an hour? How about in two hours? Eating healthy is not about being right or better or more evolved than someone else. It is about finding out what you really want in life and then organizing your entire life, including eating, to support you. Eat like your life depends on it, because it does!

What to Eat When All You Have Is a Party Store Next to Your Apartment

So you are at your apartment or dorm room and it's 3:00 pm on Saturday. You know you need to eat something because you are going to be studying for the next three hours, then meeting friends and getting pizza around 8:00 pm. You are hungry because you had a late breakfast or maybe a small lunch and all you have in the mini-fridge is a half bottle of Gatorade® and some crazy looking bread thing that you don't want to touch. You can go down to the convenience store and get something to eat, but what is the best choice? Very good question, young Jedi! Here are the questions I think you should ask yourself first.

- Do I care about how I will feel after I eat this snack?

- Do I have a craving for sweet, salty, sour or spicy   as well as general hunger?

- Am I currently well hydrated? Have I drunk enough water today?

Sometimes we are really thirsty when we think we are hungry. Our cravings are always telling us something about what we need, but we often misread the signals.

Basic Principles to Live By

1. Go for the least processed items available.

2. Avoid sugar, corn syrup and any other refined sweeteners at all costs. These will only leave you feeling foggy and whacked.

3. Nuts are usually available. Peanuts and cashews are usually stocked and almonds and sunflower seeds are often available. These are good choices to keep your blood sugar stabilized.

4. Fresh fruit, if available, is a good accompaniment to nuts. Fresh fruit by itself could send you into a less severe blood sugar spin, not anywhere near as severe as sugar, but still less than ideal for some. Fresh fruit by itself can work in the warmer months of the year if you are not terribly hungry and have eaten a good meal in the last few hours.

5. Avoid hydrogenated and partially hydrogenated oils. These are present in most chips, crackers, crunchy things and the baked goods available in convenience stores.

6. Choose foods with a simple and short list of ingredients. For example, Fritos® corn chips contain only corn, corn oil and salt. This is pretty simple. (I am in no way endorsing Fritos®, but yes, I have eaten them in a pinch. At least you know exactly what you are getting and the chemicals are missing.)

7. Cheese sticks, cheese blocks and cheese rounds are good choices, but only eat cheese from a party store if it is really cheese. This does not include cheese that you spray or that is processed. Real cheese and Fritos® will work in a pinch to keep the body fed.

8. Food bars, power bars and meal replacement bars usually contain refined sweeteners. Balance Outdoor® bars are sweetened with rice syrup and this is a better choice. If all you have to choose from is a candy bar or an energy bar, go for the energy bar.

9. Fruit juice is definitely a better choice than soda, but for some it can lead to swings in blood sugar. Juices offer concentrated carbs going into the system all at one time. The most nutritious choice is V8® or tomato juice. Grapefruit juices usually have less fruit sugar and therefore cause a less pronounced blood sugar spike and drop. Go for a 100% juice, of course.

10. Whole grain crackers (Triscuits® or Wheat Thins®) are a good choice (Triscuits® are my first preference.) Wheat Thins® have added sugar and low quality oils. Either one can work once in a while, but eat them with some nuts, nut butter or cheese.

11. Peanut butter is sometimes available, but mostly it is the kind with hydrogenated oils. If stuck between processed peanut butter and some sugar bomb "Whoo-Whoo" thing, go for the peanut butter. A much better choice is just to get some nuts. Remember, hydrogenated oils are not recommended.

12. Yogurt is usually a better choice than cheese or milk because the active cultures help digestion. (You probably need all the help you can get if you are eating meals from a convenience store!)

13. Baked rather than fried corn chips are a better choice.

14. Canned tuna is good! If you have a can opener and you need protein, grab a can of tuna and a jar of salsa. Open both, combine and eat with Fritos® or baked chips.

15. Avoid any stick made from beef or other meats. If it is made from processed meat and stuck together in a stick or strip there is probably good reason to be suspicious, especially if it is sitting in a plastic wrapper in a store. Don't eat it if you can help it.

The Short List to Remember

I recommend avoiding any foods that lead to a sugar bomb spike-and-crash. That means eating protein with whatever snack you get. My choices in order are:

- nuts
- tuna
- cheese

As filler, you can get corn chips or crackers, maybe even bread. Here are my top choices:

- baked corn chips, blue corn if available
- Fritos® corn chips
- Triscuits® or any cracker with a short ingredient list made from whole grains
- Wheat Thins®
- whole wheat bread (If it is at the average convenience store, it probably is not really whole wheat, it is part whole wheat and part refined white flour.)

When available, choose fresh fruit such as apples, bananas or oranges.

To drink, I would stick with water. Juice, if you are in need of calories to burn. My suggested options in order are:

1. water

2. V8® juice

3. tomato juice

4. grape juice (Concord grape, dark purple in color, not white grape)

5. grapefruit juice

6. orange juice

Miscellaneous food items that may also be good options include the following:

1. yogurt

2. canned fruit packed in fruit juice

3. olives and pickles (if you crave salt)

4. energy bars of all sorts, but watch out for refined sweeteners

5. other dairy products such as cottage cheese, sour cream, etc.

Here are my top combinations:

1. Fritos® and tuna with salsa

2. baked corn chips with cheese

3. Triscuits® and nuts

4. Wheat Thins® and nuts

5. apple, nuts and yogurt

6. banana, nuts, yogurt

7. cheese and apple

8. Triscuits® and tuna with salsa

Cravings

Next, it is a good idea to investigate your cravings, if you have any. The body is an intelligent system. Learning to deconstruct cravings can be really helpful. Often, times of intense study can lead us to crave sugar; the brain wants fuel. Complex carbs are the best choice. If we are under a lot of stress, protein foods help us stay strong. Protein also helps us feel assertive and alert. If you are training for baseball, lacrosse, hockey, football, basketball, track, cross-country or any other vigorous, competitive sport, you need protein to repair, build and maintain muscle.

Cravings for salt could be many things including a desire for minerals or the need to constrict energy. Every flavor is associated with a type of energy and quality in food. Every texture does the same. Begin to listen to what your body wants and respond. Those will be good choices. Pay special attention to how you feel after you eat a particular food. Remember that feeling the next time you want to eat it. If you know you feel bad, make a choice to either not feel bad or to eat it anyway and accept that you are going to feel terrible.

Finally, this list of recommendations is based on a very specific context of food availability. I do not recommend making convenience store dining your primary source of nourishment. This is about working with what you have available. Food plays a crucial role in the expression of your fullest potential.

For more information on the best foods to eat for a kick-ass life, check out www.healthyfastandcheap.com. This site is guaranteed to give you useful tips that will change the way you eat food, save money, manage your time, stay healthy and balance your energy. (It even includes tips on dating and dealing with housemates!)

I wrote this after giving a draft of Healthy, Fast and Cheap™ to Evan Fairmont, a freshman at Lewis and Clark. He told me that he enjoyed my time management tips and would use more recipes once he was out of the dorm. He also wanted to see a guide to healthy eating when all you have is access to the food options at a convenience store. A shout-out to Evan for inspiring this practical information.

What You Need to Know About Food

This is a meaningful set of principles that can support you in feeling healthy and fabulous about yourself. This report is divided into six sections and is based on six principles.

1. Emotional Eating
2. Quality of Food
3. Quantity of Food
4. The Top Five Foods to Include
5. The Top Five Worst Foods to Eat
6. The Worst Meal You Can Eat

As a Certified Holistic Health Counselor, I help my clients sort through the many conflicting dietary theories to find what works best for them. What I am offering you here are general guidelines for a healthy diet that can contribute to maintaining your optimal weight. Ultimately, you need to continue to study good health and nutrition principles and find what works for you. Here are six principles to get you started. For ongoing support and additional information you can sign up for my newsletter at www.healthyfastandcheap.com.

Principle One: Emotional Eating

- Stress
- New situations
- Social pressure

Emotional eating is basically a way to satisfy a need for nourishment. Strong feelings are experienced and food becomes a comfort for those feelings. This is not bad or wrong, but may not be the best way to get nourishment and comfort.

Causes of emotional eating:

1. **Stress.** There are three F's in the fight or flight response of stress: FLEE, FIGHT and FEED. Eating temporarily overrides low-level stress by switching your nervous system out of one state to another. However, it does not address the cause of the

previous stress and therefore it returns once you are done; only now you feel lousy from over eating too.

2. **New Situations.**   Being at school — possibly the first time you are away from home — might be overwhelming and you may be longing for comfort. You might return to comfort foods.

3. **Social Pressure.**   Ironically, the pressure to fit into a new social situation — often associated with how you look — can drive you to overeat as a way to escape the pressure to be thin or look sexy. There is nothing inherently wrong with looking good, but obsessing about it can lead you to rebel against any firm commitments you made about food.

Principle Two: Quality of Food

- Processed foods
- Whole foods
- Freshness
- Life force

The quality of the food that you eat can have a significant impact on your health. One unfortunate oversight in some mainstream nutritional theories is that little emphasis is given to quality. This is particularly significant when discussing the student diet because the quality of food often decreases in your first year in college or the first year you eat completely on your own. This can be attributed to limited availability of quality foods, dependence on the food plan, adjusting to personal responsibility and a full schedule. Here are four tips to keep in mind when looking for the best foods:

1. **Limit your intake of processed foods.** Many of the college students I interviewed were in dormitory/cafeteria food plans where the fare commonly included corn dogs, pizza and iceberg lettuce as staples. Processed foods tend to be devoid of essential nutrients and are actually taxing on the body.

2. **Increase your consumption of whole foods.** Science is catching up with traditional wisdom with the discovery of phytochemicals, glyconutrients, antioxidants, cofactors and other factors that complement the macronutrients (i.e., fats, proteins, carbohydrates).

3. **Freshness.** This is an essential element of quality that is becoming undervalued in modern America. The emphasis on freshness is maintained in many cultures around the globe and all gourmet cooking. Simply put: fresh foods are more nutritious foods. Surprisingly, many frozen vegetables and fruits retain a high nutrient density because they are packed at the peak of freshness. If any food is designed to sit on a shelf for a year, be suspicious.

4. **Life Force.** All food has a life force. This is the combination of many elements, including: freshness, growing method, whole or unprocessed, type of food, and shipping and handling. Food with a vibrant life force is clearly more energizing to our bodies. We are systems, as is our food, and we take on the quality of the system that we consume.

Principle Three: Quantity of Food

- Portion sizes
- Glycemic load
- High glycemic load foods
- Low glycemic load foods

The quantity of food is certainly an issue with respect to maintaining a healthy weight, but I tend to dig deeper than calorie counting when working with clients on sustaining health and a healthy weight. I have interviewed hundreds of people about what works or not when attempting to maintain a healthy weight and calorie counting is not always useful.

1. **Portion size is important.** Most restaurants serve up huge plates of food that are much more than you need. Portion size is even more critical when combined with time of day. I work with clients to find the optimal time of day to eat larger meals and it is generally not in the evening.

2. **Glycemic load.** Consideration of the glycemic index of foods is all the rage these days. This is a good piece of nutritional information, but it fails to take into consideration the caloric density. Those two variables are combined to create the glycemic load. The glycemic index indicates how fast food metabolizes into glucose and the caloric density shows how much glucose will be created.

3. **High glycemic load foods.** These foods have a high caloric density and turn into blood glucose rapidly. This causes excess glucose to be stored as fat and leads to hypoglycemic tendencies. Examples include: white rice, white potatoes, white sugar, fruit juice, white bread, pasta, most whole wheat breads, pastries, muffins, cookies, etc.

4. **Low glycemic load foods.** These are nutrient dense and either slow to metabolize into blood glucose or contain low carbohydrate calories or are a combination of both: e.g., green leafy vegetables (kale, collard greens, mustard greens, romaine, red leaf lettuce, etc.), turnips, carrots, parsnips (roots generally have a high glycemic index, but low glycemic load), papaya, apples, pears and grapefruit. Most water-rich fruits and vegetables are low glycemic load foods.

Principle Four: The Top Five Foods to Include

- Dark green leafy vegetables
- Papaya
- Avocado
- Cold water fish
- Blueberries

Foods to include are nutrient dense, full of life force, fresh when possible, offer a low glycemic load, contain a full spectrum of beneficial phytochemicals (plant-derived chemicals) and leave you feeling great after eating them.

1. **Dark green leafy vegetables.** This may be the number one food missing from the American diet. Look at these amazing plants and you can see the energy contained within them. Collard greens, kale and other dark green leaves are full of minerals, chlorophyll (an internal cleanser), vitamins, glyconutrients (long chain sugar molecules found in the fiber of plants) and are energetically open and expansive.

2. **Papaya.** What a great food for beauty. The flesh of a papaya is soft and smooth and contributes to your own skin looking beautiful. Just see for yourself. One of the reasons may be that papaya is rich in papain, an enzyme that assists in digestion and assimilation. There is a direct correlation between your digestive health and skin. This is mildly sweet food that has a low glycemic load and makes a great dessert.

3. **Avocado.** All you need to do is eat avocado consistently for a month to see for yourself how great this food is. It contains wonderful raw, monounsaturated fat that actually helps keep the body clean and lubricated. It's also another amazing beauty food. The low fat scare has unfortunately led to a fear of avocados, but this is completely unfounded. Good healthy fat from avocados is not only acceptable, it is essential.

4. **Cold water fish.** These aquatic animals have the highest concentration of omega-3 fatty acids DHA and EPA. Also known as EFAs (essential fatty acids), these fats contribute to a variety of beneficial effects. Most significant is a reduction in internal inflammation in all body systems. This leads to better brain function, better digestion, improved immune response, better stress management and a reduced risk of chronic disease later in life.

5. **Blueberries.** This is my favorite berry, but all berries are nutritional rock stars. They are low glycemic load foods with super high nutrient density. They taste sweet and leave you feeling clear, clean, refreshed and energized. They are absolutely loaded with beneficial phytochemicals in the form of antioxidants, flavonoids and beneficial acids. Berries are a great replacement snack for other sweet foods.

Principle Five: The Top Five Worst Foods to Eat

- Hydrogenated oils
- Sugar, corn syrup, sucrose, dextrose, fructose, etc.
- White flour
- Refined salt
- Fast food

1. The more a food is processed, the more chance it has of having a negative impact on your health. I don't believe that there are bad foods, but hydrogenated oils are not food, they are molecular structures not found in nature.

2. Although I don't believe that any foods are bad, I certainly think that there are better, higher quality options for satisfying a craving for sweet foods. Refined sweeteners, as I mentioned above, hit the bloodstream fast and furious and lead to stored fat and a cycle of cravings based on low blood sugar. (The body quickly makes massive amounts of insulin when you eat a lot of sugar, storea what it cannot immediately use, and then it is left with excess insulin. Because the body wants immediate fuel but has nothing in the bloodstream to serve this role, you crave more sugar.)

3. White flour metabolizes like sugar.

4. Salt is sodium chloride and sodium is an essential mineral. But sodium is only one of many important minerals and when consumed in excess, especially in the absence of other minerals, it causes an internal imbalance. A high quality, unrefined sea salt will contain trace minerals that work to maintain better balance in the body.

5. Fast food usually combines hydrogenated oils, corn syrup, white flour and refined salt. This gives a meal lacking in life force, nutrient density, mineral profile and clean fuel. The meat in fast food, though low quality, tends to carry the meal because even low quality meat is a source of minerals, vitamins and energy.

In the documentary *Super Size Me*, Morgan Spurlock demonstrates the dangers of excessive fast foods consumption by eating nothing but McDonald's for a month. He gained nearly 30 pounds, his liver became very toxic and he went through periods of depression.

Principle Six: The Worst Meal You Can Eat

Danish and Coffee

Pastry and coffee is a common breakfast, snack and sometimes even a meal for many people. It is fast, easy to consume and gives you an immediate lift. Part of that is due to the rapid assimilation of sugars into the bloodstream, which gives the brain an uptake of feel-good chemicals. The other aspect of the immediate lift is the obvious effect of caffeine. The down side to this injection diet — referring to the way that we commonly use these foods as a boost or lift — is dramatic.

Pastry is a high glycemic load food that leads to a blood sugar surge, storage as fat and then a crash. The crash leads to further cravings for sugar and this leads to a chronic cycle that begins to disrupt the balance in the body. The prolonged use of caffeine over-stimulates the adrenal glands and, over time, also contributes to hormone imbalances in the body. The long-term cumulative effects can be thyroid problems, adrenal fatigue, lowered immune response, depression, menstrual irregularities and lowered sexual response in men and women.

This is just the beginning of the Integrative Nutrition approach to healthy weight. For more free information, see postings from my blog at www.healthyfastandcheap.com.

Healthy, Fast and Cheap™ Target Diet

The basic approach for eating Healthy, Fast and Cheap™ is outlined in this diagram.

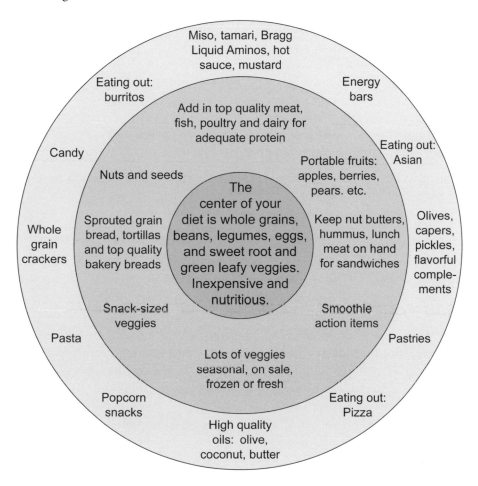

Miso, tamari, Bragg Liquid Aminos, hot sauce, mustard

Eating out: burritos

Energy bars

Add in top quality meat, fish, poultry and dairy for adequate protein

Candy

Eating out: Asian

Nuts and seeds

Portable fruits: apples, berries, pears. etc.

The center of your diet is whole grains, beans, legumes, eggs, and sweet root and green leafy veggies. Inexpensive and nutritious.

Sprouted grain bread, tortillas and top quality bakery breads

Keep nut butters, hummus, lunch meat on hand for sandwiches

Olives, capers, pickles, flavorful comple- ments

Whole grain crackers

Snack-sized veggies

Smoothie action items

Pasta

Pastries

Lots of veggies seasonal, on sale, frozen or fresh

Popcorn snacks

Eating out: Pizza

High quality oils: olive, coconut, butter

The Big Picture

Your diet, budget and time fit into the bigger picture of your life. For most people, food, time and money are part of some other greater organizing principles. We eat to live, not live to eat, though you can be damn sure that I'm here to enjoy food too!

If you are eating foods that keep you half alive out of habit, you are spending way more than you need to at restaurants. If it seems easier or you just don't know where to begin to cook at home, then take a look at what you get and what you lose. Become very clear about the plus side and the minus side of what you eat and the way you eat. Maybe you'll find that donuts and pastries for breakfast really are important to you and you will trade that experience for the high energy of a super food smoothie. Then it is done. No guilt, no regret. ENJOY!

Or maybe you can clarify how much money you will save each month if you pack a lunch each day and that a laptop upgrade is more important than eating at the food court.

This whole thing is not about being good or bad in the health choices that you make. It is about making choices and living in a way that supports your purpose.

It is not about obsessing over food!

This cookbook offers you time- and money-saving tips. It is offered with a spirit of mindfulness and quality. It comes out of a "both/and," not an "either/or" paradigm. You can enjoy the process of making food and make efficient use of your time. You can enjoy food and get the best nutrition.

Get Into It

Dips

Snacks

Popcorn & Nuts

Fruit Snacks

Leaving Home Cookbook
and Survival Guide

Get Into It Contents

Be Ready

One of the best things you can do for snacks or any meal for that matter is to have your favorite healthy and quick foods on hand, ready for a quick meal or snack. The coffee and doughnut routine can keep you going for a while, but over time it is a sure fire way to knock down your vitality. If you don't have the right foods available in your kitchen, then you can be sure the wrong foods will end up in your belly every time!

Dips

Black Bean Salsa

1 (15 ounce) can black beans, drained
4 - 6 green onions with tops, diced
½ - ¾ cup snipped fresh cilantro leaves
1 - 2 cloves garlic, minced
1 tablespoon canola oil
1 teaspoon fresh lime juice

▶ Mix all ingredients in bowl and refrigerate before serving. Yields about 2 cups.

TIP: It's easier to cut cilantro with scissors than with a knife.

Easy Gringo Guacamole

3 ripe avocados, peeled, seeded
1 tablespoon lemon juice
1 teaspoon minced garlic
1 small tomato, chopped
¼ cup hot salsa
Corn chips

▶ Place all ingredients in blender or food processor and pulse 2 to 3 times. Add 1 teaspoon salt and a little pepper.

▶ Process until guacamole is chunky, but not pureed. Serve with corn chips. Yields 1 cup.

Confetti Dip

1 (15 ounce) can whole kernel corn, drained
1 (15 ounce) can black beans, drained
1 tablespoon olive oil
1 tablespoon vinegar
1 teaspoon dry basil
1 (16 ounce) jar salsa

▶ Combine all ingredients and a little sea salt and pepper in bowl and mix well. Refrigerate for several hours before serving. Serve with chips. Yields 3 cups.

TIP: Unpasteurized apple cider vinegar is a good one to use.

Frijoles Refritos

Refried Beans. These are just recycled pinto beans with some other stuff in 'em. See A Basic Pot of Beans on page 158 to cook the beans.

Leftover cooked pinto beans
Butter
Shredded cheddar cheese

▶ Cook leftover beans in saucepan until most or all of liquid is gone. Drain any excess liquid and mash remaining beans.

▶ Fry mashed beans in large, heavy skillet with butter until mixture is hot.

▶ Serve immediately with cheese on top.

TIP: If you wanted to get fancy, you could add chili powder, cumin, minced onion and/or chopped jalapenos.

Vegetable Dive

You will have everyone saying, "You mean this is spinach?"

1 (10 ounce) package frozen chopped spinach, thawed, drained
2 cubes rapunzel bouillon
2 (8 ounce) cartons sour cream
1 bunch fresh green onions with tops, chopped
1 tablespoon lemon juice
Chips

▶ Squeeze spinach between paper towels to completely remove excess moisture.

▶ Mix bouillon cubes with sour cream in bowl and mash them until they mix thoroughly. (You gotta make sure the bouillon is dissolved or you get these pockets of really intense salty flavor.)

▶ Combine all ingredients in medium bowl. (Several drops of hot sauce is also good.) Cover and refrigerate.

▶ Mix once more before serving. Serve with chips. Yields 2 cups.

Creamy Onion Dip

2 (8 ounce) packages cream cheese, softened
3 tablespoons lemon juice
1 tablespoon dried onion flakes or onion powder
¼ teaspoon garlic powder
1 tablespoon tamari, optional
1 (8 ounce) carton sour cream

▶ Beat cream cheese in bowl until smooth. Blend in lemon juice, onion flakes, garlic and tamari.

▶ Gradually fold in sour cream until it blends well. Refrigerate. Serve with chips, crackers or fresh vegetables. Yields 3 cups.

Five-Minute Dip

1 (8 ounce) package cream cheese, softened
1 cup mayonnaise
1 tablespoon tamari, optional
¼ teaspoon garlic powder
¼ teaspoon onion powder
½ onion, finely minced
Fresh vegetables

▶ Combine cream cheese and mayonnaise in bowl and beat until creamy.

▶ Stir in spices and onion. Refrigerate and serve with fresh vegetables. Yields 2 cups.

Party Shrimp Dip

1 (8 ounce) package cream cheese, softened
½ cup mayonnaise
1 (6 ounce) can tiny, cooked shrimp, drained
¾ teaspoon Creole seasoning
Chips

▶ Beat cream cheese and mayonnaise in bowl. Stir in shrimp and seasoning. Mix well and refrigerate. Serve with chips. Yields 2 cups.

TIP: Creole seasoning is really good on steamed vegetables and chicken.

Tamari is a salty, earthy condiment made from soybeans. A lot of supermarket soy sauce is made from isolated soy protein and caramel color and is not a healthy choice. Look for a good quality fermented soy sauce like Eden® Foods brand.

Hot Cheese Dip

1 large onion, chopped
¼ cup (½ stick) butter
1 (10 ounce) can tomatoes and green chilies
1 (16 ounce) package cubed cheddar cheese
Chips

▶ Saute onion in butter in saucepan, add tomatoes and green chilies and stir while cooking. Add cheese gradually to onion-tomato mixture.

▶ Heat and stir on medium until cheese melts. Serve hot with chips. Yields 2 cups.

TIP: The trick for melting cheese well is to keep the heat low enough and to stir frequently until it reaches desired consistency.

Fruit Dunk

4 ounces cashews
1 (8 ounce) package cream cheese, softened
4 ounces brown rice syrup
¼ teaspoon ground cinnamon
⅛ teaspoon ground ginger
Sliced fruit with peels (apples, pears, kiwi, nectarines, peaches)

▶ Soak cashews in water for 30 minutes and drain.

▶ Place cashews, cream cheese, rice syrup, cinnamon and ginger in blender and process until ingredients mix. Refrigerate.

▶ Serve with slices of nectarines or any other fruit with peels. Yields 2 cups.

Lucky Black-Eyed Pea Scoop

2 (15 ounce) cans black-eyed peas, drained
1 small onion, chopped
1 teaspoon minced garlic
1 (10 ounce) can tomatoes and green chilies, drained
Corn chips

▶ Combine peas, onion, garlic, and tomatoes and green chilies in bowl and mix.

▶ Serve with corn chips. Yields 4 cups.

TIP: *If you don't have fresh garlic or don't want to buy it, just use ½ teaspoon garlic powder or garlic salt.*

Spinach-Feta Dip

1 (8 ounce) carton sour cream
1 (8 ounce) package cream cheese, softened
¾ cup crumbled feta cheese
1 (10 ounce) package frozen chopped spinach, thawed, drained well

▶ Beat sour cream, cream cheese and 1 teaspoon salt in bowl. Fold in feta cheese.

▶ Squeeze spinach between paper towels to completely remove excess moisture. Stir into cheese mixture. Add 1 teaspoon minced garlic, if you like. Yields 3 cups.

Steamy Hot Artichoke Dip

1 (14 ounce) can artichoke hearts, drained, chopped
1¼ cups mayonnaise (not light)
1 cup grated parmesan cheese
2 teaspoons minced garlic
Wheat crackers

▶ Preheat oven to 350°.

▶ Combine artichoke, mayonnaise, parmesan and garlic in bowl and mix well.

▶ Spoon into 8 or 9-inch glass pie pan and bake for 25 minutes. Serve hot with wheat crackers. Yields about 3 cups.

Snacks

1st Some Quick Morning Snacks

- An apple and a bag of raw or roasted almonds.

- A couple of celery sticks, carrots and a bag of cashews.

- Quick oats with raisins and sunflower seeds. (All you need to do is boil water and pour this over the quick oats in a bowl with a serving of whey protein mixed in.)

- A cup of yogurt and some trail mix.

- Toast with PBJ.

- Green tea.

It's easy to get up and put water on to boil. Come back when you've done some of your morning routine: don't worry, the water won't burn so there is no need to keep track of time within reason, you don't want to burn the pan! The boiling water can be used for quick oats or added to a travel mug with a tea bag.

As for toast, I recommend Food for Life sprouted grain bread. This is fabulous toasted and is packed with protein and complex carbohydrates. (More on this later.)

Cheddar-Butter Toast

½ cup (1 stick) butter, softened
1¼ cups shredded cheddar cheese
1 teaspoon Worcestershire sauce
¼ teaspoon garlic powder
Sprouted grain or sourdough bread

▶ Combine all ingredients in bowl and spread on sprouted grain or thick-sliced sourdough bread.

▶ Turn on broiler to preheat. When oven is hot, turn off broiler and put toast in oven for about 15 minutes. Serves 4.

Peanut Butter Spread

1 (8 ounce) package cream cheese, softened
1⅔ cups peanut butter
½ cup raw honey
Apple wedges or graham crackers

▶ Beat all ingredients in bowl. Serve with apple wedges, celery sticks or whole grain crackers or bread. Yields 3 cups.

TIP: *You can do this with almond butter or any other nut butter. You could even make your own nut butter. Throw 2 cups almonds or cashews into a food processor and blend until smooth; add the remaining ingredients. Yeah, Baby!*

Cheese Drops

2 cups whole wheat biscuit mix* or biscuit mix
⅓ cup sour cream
1 egg
1 (4 ounce) can chopped green chilies, drained
1½ cups shredded sharp cheddar cheese

▶ Preheat oven to 375°.

▶ Combine biscuit mix, sour cream, egg and green chilies in bowl and mix until they blend well. Stir in cheese. (Mixture will be thick.)

▶ Drop heaping teaspoonfuls of dough onto sprayed baking sheet. Bake for 10 minutes or until golden brown. Serve warm. Serves 4 to 6.

*TIP: *I like Arrowhead Mills and Bob's Red Mill®. Check for availability. Watch out for mixes with hydrogenated oil and refined flours.*

Quick Cheesy Broccoli Quesadillas

1 (8 ounce) package organic shredded cheddar cheese
1 (10 ounce) package frozen chopped broccoli, drained*
⅓ cup salsa
8 (6 inch) sprouted grain tortillas
I teaspoon coconut oil or organic butter for pan

▶ Combine cheese, broccoli and salsa in bowl and mix well. Spoon about ¼ cup cheese-broccoli mixture onto 1 side of each tortilla and fold tortilla over filling.

▶ Add coconut oil or butter to skillet and cook 2 quesadillas at a time on medium heat. Cook for about 3 minutes on both sides or until tortillas are light brown. Serves 4.

*TIP: Squeeze broccoli between paper towels to completely remove excess moisture.

Shrimp Squares Deluxe

1 (6 ounce) can shrimp, drained, chopped
1 cup mayonnaise
1 cup shredded cheddar cheese
10 - 12 slices sprouted grain bread, trimmed

▶ Preheat broiler.

▶ Combine shrimp, mayonnaise and cheese in bowl. Spread shrimp mixture on bread squares and broil until bubbly. Cut into 4 squares. Serves 8 to 10.

Sardines are rich in omega-3 fatty acids, calcium, protein and vitamin D and are good for the brain. Eat them right out of the can with crackers any time, anywhere.

Potato Skins

4 baking potatoes
1 cup shredded cheddar cheese
4 - 6 slices bacon, fried crisp, drained, crumbled

▶ Slice potatoes lengthwise and bake for 30 minutes.

▶ Scoop out potato, leaving ¼ inch skins, and fill each potato skin with cheese and bacon.

▶ Place on baking dish and broil for 3 minutes or until cheese melts. Yields 8 halves.

TIP: You can use the scooped out potatoes to add to soup, fry with free-range eggs in the morning or make mashed potatoes!

Tortilla Rollers

1 (8 ounce) package cream cheese, softened
1 (4 ounce) can chopped black olives, drained
1 (4 ounce) can chopped green chilies, drained
1 (12 ounce) jar salsa, divided
½ cup finely chopped kale
Sprouted grain tortillas

▶ Beat cream cheese in bowl until smooth. Add olives, green chilies, ¼ cup salsa and kale to cream cheese and mix well.

▶ Spread cream cheese mixture on flour tortillas and roll. Refrigerate for several hours.

▶ Cut tortilla rolls into ½-inch slices, insert toothpick in each slice and serve with remaining salsa for dipping. Serves 4.

www.mercola.com is the highest-ranking Web site on the Internet for integrative health resources.

Taste-Tempting Hot Squares

1 cup grated parmesan cheese
1 cup shredded mozzarella cheese
2 (14 ounce) cans artichoke hearts, drained, chopped
1 (8 ounce) carton chive and onion cream cheese
2 (8 ounce) packages refrigerated crescent rolls

▶ Preheat oven to 350°.

▶ Combine parmesan cheese, mozzarella cheese, chopped artichokes and cream cheese in bowl and beat until they blend well.

▶ Unroll both packages of dough and press into sprayed 10 x 15-inch baking pan in rectangular shape. Seal seams and perforations.

▶ Spread with artichoke mixture. Bake for 20 minutes or until crust is light golden brown. Cut into squares to serve. Serves 6 to 8.

Tuna Melt Bites

1 (10 ounce) package frozen spinach, drained
2 (6 ounce) cans white tuna in water, drained, flaked
¼ cup miso
¼ cup olive oil
1½ cups shredded mozzarella cheese, divided
Rye or whole wheat crackers*

▶ Preheat oven to 350°.

▶ Squeeze spinach between paper towels to completely remove excess moisture. Combine spinach, tuna, miso, olive oil and 1 cup cheese in large bowl and mix well.

▶ Spoon into sprayed pie pan and bake for 15 minutes.

▶ Remove from oven and sprinkle remaining cheese over top. Return to oven and bake for additional 5 minutes. Serves 4.

*TIP: I like Ryvita thin rye crackers and Ak-Mak® whole wheat crackers. If you can't get those, Triscuits® will do the job.

Spinach-Stuffed Mushrooms

1 (8 ounce) package frozen spinach, thawed
2 eggs, beaten
1 heaping tablespoon nutritional yeast
¼ teaspoon garlic powder
½ teaspoon sea salt
24 large mushrooms, stems removed
½ cup shredded cheddar cheese

▶ Preheat oven to 375°.

▶ Squeeze spinach between paper towels to completely remove excess moisture.

▶ Mix spinach, eggs, nutritional yeast, garlic powder, sea salt and ¼ teaspoon pepper.

▶ Arrange mushroom caps on lightly sprayed baking sheet. Spoon 1 teaspoon spinach mix into each mushroom cap and top with ½ teaspoon cheese.

▶ Bake for 20 minutes. Serves 6 to 8.

TIP: *Nutritional yeast is super high in protein and B-vitamins. You can add it to soups, sandwiches, popcorn, rice, veggies or even toast. It has a nutty flavor.*

Chicken Wings

3 pounds chicken wings
1 (10 ounce) bottle teriyaki sauce

▶ Rinse wings and drain.

▶ Place chicken wings in 9 x 13-inch glass dish or pan, pour teriyaki sauce over pieces and turn to coat. Marinate wings for 24 hours in refrigerator and turn several times.

▶ When ready to bake, preheat oven to 250°.

▶ Remove from refrigerator and let stand for 15 minutes. Pour off most of sauce and discard.

▶ Cover and bake for 2 hours. Uncover during last 15 minutes of baking time to brown wings. Serves 4.

TIP: *There are lots of marinades in the grocery stores, but check the ingredient lists and avoid high fructose corn syrup, soybean oil, hydrolyzed proteins, monosodium glutamate and anything with lots of sugar in general.*

Chicken Wing Sauce:

You can make your own sauce by combining the following:

6 ounces soy sauce or tamari or Bragg Liquid Aminos
1 tablespoon fresh grated ginger or 1 teaspoon powdered ginger
1 garlic clove, minced or 1 teaspoon garlic powder
1 ounce toasted sesame oil
1 ounce maple syrup
1 ounce brown rice vinegar
Optional red pepper for heat (cayenne, Tabasco® sauce, chile, your preference)

No-Fuss Meatballs

Great Healthy, Fast and Cheap™ party food for watching the game!

2 (16 ounce) packages ground buffalo or lean ground beef
2 leftover slices bread, dry
1 tablespoon tamari
1 teaspoon garlic powder
½ teaspoon celery salt

▶ Preheat oven to 350°.

▶ Mix buffalo with all ingredients in bowl and roll all into small balls. Place on sprayed baking sheet and bake for 25 minutes.

▶ Cool and place in large freezer bags and freeze. When needed, remove meatballs from freezer and prepare sauce. Serves 4.

Sauce:

1 tablespoon soy sauce
½ cup chili sauce
⅔ cup grape or plum jelly
¼ cup dijon-style mustard

▶ Cook meatballs with soy sauce in skillet until hot. Combine chili sauce, jelly and mustard in bowl and pour over meatballs.

▶ Cook and stir until jelly dissolves and mixture comes to boil. Reduce heat, cover and simmer for about 5 minutes. Be sure to have toothpicks ready for serving.

Papaya is in the top five best foods to eat. One of the reasons may be that papaya is rich in papain, an enzyme that assists in digestion and assimilation. There is a direct correlation between your digestive health and your skin.

Popcorn & Nuts

The All-Time Best
Student Snack Food: Popcorn!

Popcorn is so easy to make and so cheap — not to mention healthy — that it is silly not to include it. With a little practice, you can master this technique.

 ## Perfect Popcorn

▶ Heat coconut oil on high heat in a pot. (You should use a stainless steel pot or a really good non-stick pan. I use the non-stick option for this most of the time.) Make sure the oil almost covers the bottom of the pot.

▶ After the oil begins to flow more freely due to the heat, add 3 popcorn kernels.

▶ After these pop, add popcorn to just about cover the bottom of the pot and cover with lid.

▶ Allow popcorn a few minutes to heat and gently toss occasionally.

▶ Once popcorn starts to pop, continue to toss kernels more vigorously.

▶ After the last few kernels have popped, pour the popcorn into a bowl.

▶ Pour some olive oil in the hot pan and then drizzle this over the popcorn.

▶ Sprinkle with nutritional yeast and adobo or another finely ground salt.

Total cooking and clean-up time is under 10 minutes. A 1-pound bag of organic popcorn is under $2. That's a lot of popcorn!

Popcorn-Peanut Treats

⅔ cup peanut butter
½ cup honey
1 cup granola cereal
1 cup roasted salted peanuts
3 cups popped popcorn

▶ Mix peanut butter and honey in saucepan until it melts. Add granola and peanuts and stir.

▶ Add popcorn and toss gently to spread as much peanut butter as possible.

▶ Scrape bowl into baking dish and pat down gently to even out top. Cut into squares when cool. Serves 6 to 8.

Popcorn Party Mix

1 cup chow mein noodles
½ cup peanuts
⅓ cup peanut oil
2 tablespoons teriyaki sauce
¾ teaspoon salt or sea salt
½ teaspoon garlic powder
½ teaspoon cayenne pepper
⅛ teaspoon honey
2½ quarts popped popcorn

▶ Preheat oven to 275°.

▶ Mix all ingredients except popcorn in small saucepan, stir well over low heat and remove when warm. Place popcorn in large bowl and pour sauce over popcorn. Toss gently to coat pieces.

▶ Pour popcorn into large roasting pan and bake for 15 minutes. Cool slightly before eating. Yields 2½ quarts.

TV Popcorn Bites

1 cup honey
1 tablespoon lemon juice
4 quarts popped popcorn

▶ Preheat oven to 275°.

▶ Combine honey, ½ cup water and lemon juice in small saucepan and cook over high heat until mixture boils and reaches hard-ball stage.

▶ Pour over popcorn and toss to spread honey. Pour into baking pan or cookie sheet and spread out.

▶ Bake for about 10 minutes. Stir and turn popcorn pieces. Bake for additional 10 minutes. Yields 4 quarts.

Barbecued Walnuts

3 tablespoons butter, melted
¼ cup Worcestershire sauce
3 dashes hot sauce
2 tablespoons tomato paste
1 teaspoon maple syrup
5 cups walnut halves

▶ Preheat oven to 400°.

▶ Combine butter, Worcestershire sauce, hot sauce, tomato paste, maple syrup and a little touch of salt in bowl and mix well. Pour over walnut halves and stir until all walnuts are well coated.

▶ Bake in 9 x 13-inch baking pan and stir every 5 minutes for 20 minutes. Remove from oven and pour walnuts out on 2 layers of paper towels. Cool to room temperature. Yields 5 cups.

Roasted Mixed Nuts

1 pound mixed nuts
¼ cup maple syrup
1 teaspoon garlic powder
1 teaspoon onion powder
1 tablespoon tamari

▶ Preheat oven to 300°.

▶ Combine nuts and maple syrup in bowl and mix well. Sprinkle garlic powder, onion powder and tamari and stir gently to coat.

▶ Spread in sprayed 10 x 15-inch baking pan. Bake for 25 minutes or until light brown and cool. Yields 1 pound.

Slivered Garlic Peanuts

Coconut oil
2 pounds shelled, skinned raw peanuts*
6 - 7 heads (55 - 60 cloves) garlic, peeled, sliced thinly

▶ Heat enough oil on medium-high in wok or skillet to cover peanuts; add peanuts. Stir peanuts constantly and cook until peanuts begin to brown.

▶ Turn heat to simmer, stir constantly and cook until peanuts turn golden brown. (Do not burn.) Drain peanuts in strainer and cool.

▶ Heat enough oil on medium-high in wok or skillet to cover garlic; add garlic. Stir garlic constantly and cook until it is translucent.

▶ Turn heat to simmer, stir constantly and cook until garlic is crispy. (Do not burn.) Drain garlic in strainer, cool and mix with peanuts. Salt to taste. Serve immediately. Store in sealed container. Yields 2 pounds.

*TIP: *You can buy raw peanuts already shelled and skinned. Don't think you have to do this step from scratch.*

Fruit Snacks

1st Baked Apples

A great way to get sophisticated without a lot of work.

3 Granny Smith apples
Handful of oats
Handful of raisins
Ground cinnamon
Maple syrup

▶ Preheat oven to 325°.

▶ Cut out core of apple with paring knife. Stuff some oats and raisins into the apple and sprinkle with cinnamon.

▶ Bake for 15 minutes in sprayed baking dish.

▶ Remove and lightly drizzle with maple syrup. Return to oven and broil for 2 minutes or until brown on top. Serves 3.

TIP: *Enjoy this with whole milk organic yogurt for dessert!*

Get-Up-and-Go Crunch

1 (6 ounce) carton fruit-flavored yogurt
⅓ cup whole grain cereal
½ cup fruit (strawberries, blueberries, raspberries)

▶ Pour half of yogurt, cereal and fruit in tall glass. Repeat layers and enjoy a great breakfast! Serves 1.

TIP: *I don't recommend eating cereal often, but it can be a quick way to get breakfast. Look for cereals without added sugar like shredded wheat and Grape-Nuts® or very little sugar like Cheerios®.*

Guava is a tropical fruit loaded with more potassium than a banana, more lycopene (antioxidant) than tomatoes and is the ultimate high fiber food with 9 grams of fiber in 1 cup.

Banana-Apple Crunch Time

2 large apples
1 - 2 tablespoons butter
1 banana
Ground cinnamon
1 tablespoon maple syrup
1 (8 ounce) carton plain yogurt
1 cup granola

▶ Chop apple into slices and saute in butter in skillet for 5 minutes.

▶ Add banana and saute for additional 2 minutes

▶ Dust with cinnamon and mix in maple syrup and remove to cool.

▶ Combine yogurt and granola or cereal in small bowl. Pour apples into 2 small bowls or mugs and top with yogurt mixture. Serves 2.

TIP: *Organic foods are always better and we recommend organic butter and organic plain whole milk yogurt when you can afford it. Granola is often considered a healthy food, but can be loaded with sugar and low quality oils. While whole grains are part of the Healthy, Fast and Cheap™ lifestyle, you want to make sure to sidestep lots of added sugar and especially hydrogenated (or partially hydrogenated) oils.*

Granola sweetened with honey, molasses, maple syrup or rice syrup is much better than cereals loaded with sugars.

Wake Up

Beverages

Smoothies

Cereals

Eggs

**Waffles, Pancakes
& French Toast**

Breads

Leaving Home Cookbook
and Survival Guide

Wake Up Contents

Cool, Clear Water

When you think about it, water is the ultimate Healthy, Fast and Cheap™ drink. Soda, coffee, juice and tea do not hydrate as well as water, despite a study to the contrary paid for by soft drink companies.

Don't buy it!

Soft drinks do not hydrate like water. In fact, anything with caffeine actually dries out the body and you have to drink even more water! Juice is not so bad, but not nearly as good as water. Juice is food first, hydration second.

The body is mostly water and has complex systems to keep every cell in balance. Dehydration can lead to constipation, congestion, dry and irritated sinus and lung tissue, fatigue, clouded thinking and more.

Think about it. If you have ever run for a while, played a long game of basketball, volleyball, football or any other extended sport and have gone without drinking, you know that dehydration reduces physical performance.

The average recommendation for water is eight glasses a day. That is a good target, but you will need more water if you live in Phoenix than you would if you lived in Seattle. Makes sense, right? You need more water if you are exercising for an extended amount of time. If you eat more protein, you need more water. More salt? More water.

And finally, water is the first thing to check out if you are having cravings. **The biggest cause of cravings is dehydration.** So the next time you feel a craving for something sweet, try having a glass of water, you may just be thirsty!

Beverages

Cafe Latte

Half-and-half cream or milk
Freshly brewed coffee

▶ Heat ½ cup cream or milk in small saucepan, but do not boil. Pour into coffee mug and fill with coffee. Use sweetener of your choice. (You don't have to make froth for the top to have cafe latte.)

1st Mate Latte

Enjoy the buzz!

1 tablespoon or 1 tea bag mate
½ cup milk
¼ teaspoon vanilla
Dash ground cinnamon
1 tablespoon honey

▶ Brew mate tea according to package directions in 1 cup water. Heat milk in saucepan, but do not boil.

▶ Blend tea and milk with vanilla, cinnamon and honey on high until frothy. Serves 1.

Quick Cappuccino

2 cups organic milk
1 tablespoon honey
2 cups strong, hot, freshly brewed coffee
Ground cinnamon or nutmeg

▶ Heat milk and honey in small pot, but do not boil. Pour into blender and process until frothy.

▶ Pour hot coffee in mugs and pour froth over top of each. Sprinkle cinnamon or nutmeg on top. Serves 2 to 3.

TIP: *Here is a great way to save money and go organic at the same time. If you are used to shelling out $4 a pop for tricked-out coffee, just make this at home with high quality organic ingredients. Save money. Eat better. It will take about as much time as it takes to walk into the coffee shop, stand in line, run your debit card and walk out. Maybe even quicker!*

Spiced Coffee or Tea

1 cup freshly brewed coffee or tea
1 teaspoon grated lemon peel
1 teaspoon ground cinnamon
¼ teaspoon ground cloves

▶ Pour hot coffee or tea, lemon peel, cinnamon and cloves into coffee cup and sweeten to taste. Serves 1.

Quick and Easy Hot Cocoa

If you can get it, use raw cacao powder for a righteous blast of cacao goodness.

1 cup milk
1 tablespoon cacao or cocoa powder
1 tablespoon honey
¼ cup milk or cream, optional

▶ Heat milk in saucepan, but do not boil. Add cacao, honey and whip. Serves 1.

TIP: This is especially good with coconut milk!

 # Classic Chai

2 teaspoons black tea or 2 tea bags
¼ cup fresh ginger or 1 tablespoon powdered ginger
8 cardamom pods
3 sticks cinnamon
2 star anise
8 whole cloves
8 peppercorns or 1 teaspoon black pepper

▶ Bring 3 cups water to a boil in saucepan and add ingredients except black tea.

▶ Simmer for 10 minutes, then turn off heat and add black tea.

▶ Strain into mug. Enjoy with milk and honey. Serves 2.

Lemonade Tea

Juice of 4 lemons
4 tea bags
¼ cup maple syrup
1 quart sparkling water, chilled

▶ Steep tea in 3 quarts water and mix with maple syrup and lemon juice. Add sparkling water just before serving. Serves 10 to 12.

Instant Spiced Tea Mix

1 (9 ounce) jar instant Tang®
½ cup instant lemonade mix
1½ cups sugar
1 cup instant tea mix
2 teaspoons ground cinnamon
1 teaspoon ground cloves

▶ Combine all ingredients in large bowl and mix well. Store in sealed container and shake well before using.

▶ Use about 1 tablespoon per cup of boiling water. Yields about 30 to 40 cups of tea.

TIP: *Mixture can be stored for about 8 months.*

Rooibos Chai

2 tablespoons or 2 tea bags rooibos tea
¼ cup fresh ginger or 1 tablespoon powdered ginger
8 cardamom pods
3 sticks cinnamon
2 star anise
8 whole cloves
8 peppercorns or 1 teaspoon black pepper

▶ Bring 2 cups water in saucepan to a boil and add all ingredients. Simmer for 10 minutes. Enjoy with milk and honey. Serves 2.

Hot Cranberry Drink

1½ quarts cranberry juice
1 (12 ounce) can frozen orange juice concentrate, thawed
½ teaspoon ground cinnamon

▶ Combine cranberry juice, orange juice and 1½ orange juice cans water in large saucepan. Bring to boil to blend flavors.

▶ Add cinnamon and stir well. Serve hot. Serves 6 to 8.

TIP: *Make sure cranberry juice is sweetened with fruit juice, not high fructose corn syrup.*

Mulled Apple Cider

2 quarts apple cider or apple juice
2 teaspoons whole cloves
2 teaspoons allspice
6 sticks cinnamon

▶ Combine all ingredients in large saucepan. Heat for
15 to 20 minutes over low heat and serve immediately.
Serves 8 to 10.

*TIP: Expect apple cider to be cloudy. The best cider is almost pulpy.
Use apple juice only when you absolutely cannot find cider.*

Best Tropical Punch

1 (46 ounce) can pineapple juice
1 (46 ounce) can apricot nectar (no sugar added)
Juice of 8 limes
¼ cup finely grated ginger
3 quarts sparkling water, chilled

▶ Combine pineapple juice, apricot nectar and lime juice in pitcher.
Wrap grated ginger in fine cloth and squeeze juice into fruit
juices. Refrigerate.

▶ When ready to serve, add sparkling water. Serves 14 to 16.

*TIP: If you want this even sweeter than the juice provides (which is
already too sweet for me), you can add a spot of maple syrup,
agave nectar or stevia. Be CAREFUL with the stevia! (Stevia is
VERY sweet.)*

 # 1st Healthy Soda

Sparkling water, club soda or carbonated water
100% fruit juice concentrate

▶ Mix 1 (16 ounce) glass of sparkling water with
1 tablespoon of fruit juice concentrate. You can
also use fresh squeezed juice, just use a little more!

Breakfast

It is said that breakfast is the most important meal of the day and for good reason. If you are currently skipping breakfast, STOP! Metabolically, this is like turning the key in a car and trying to drive without gas. Eating breakfast is essential because it sets your metabolism in motion. This does not mean, however, that you need to eat a full breakfast of cereal, fruit, eggs, hash browns, toast, sausage and bacon each morning when you wake up. This is over the top. Breakfast is important but so, too, is moderation!

What you need are quick, high-energy foods to sustain you. We're all different, so for some fruit and yogurt will be great; others will do well with whole grain hot cereal and still others will thrive on eggs or high protein drinks. Your preferences will also likely change with the season, your level of activity, or as a result of stress or illness. Learn to read your own body's signals.

The most important thing you can do with your breakfast is to get it into your belly! I have therefore included some strategies to help you maximize your time and make you more efficient in the mornings.

NOTE: Most of us are usually very conservative in our selection of breakfast foods. Go ahead and break out of the mold. Try something other than cereal, toast, cold pizza and other traditional breakfast foods. Salad for breakfast? Why not?

Smoothies

This is the ultimate breakfast food for the student.

You will need a blender or a food processor, a selection of frozen and fresh fruit, milk (organic cow's milk, goat's milk, soy milk, rice milk, almond milk, etc.), juice or water and your favorite "boosts".

I like to add a protein source and some kind of green food powder. It's nice to have couple of bags of frozen bananas on hand in the warmer months.

If you are a big smoothie fan, you can also get perfectly good produce cheap, even if it looks a little too ripe. Establish a friendship with the produce staff at your local market and ask them for any overripe or bruised fruit that you can use for smoothies. They may give it to you for free or for a substantial discount!

Character

Strawberry, blueberry, apple, peach, grapes, mango, papaya, spinach, cherries, plums, raspberries and pineapple.

Smoothness

Milk, including: organic cow's, goat's, soy, oat, almond, rice and coconut. (Coconut water can be used as well. In fact, I recommend coconut water or milk as my first choice.) Orange, apple and/or grape juice can also be used, but I recommend using fruit juices in moderation because they are a concentrated source of simple sugars. They contribute to a sharp rise then a fall in blood sugar, and they don't promote sustained energy.

Boosts

Protein powder (whey, soy, rice), flax seed/oil, powdered green drink (spirulina, wheat grass, barley grass, chlorella, etc.), cacao (or raw cacao), goji berry, bee pollen, acai, acerola powder (a rich source of vitamin C) and ginseng.

Flavors

Vanilla, cinnamon, ginger and cocoa powder.

Sweetener: really raw honey (#1 source of enzymes ever), maple syrup, agave nectar.

You can buy a bus load of cheap bananas if you get them when they are over-ripe at the grocery store. Bring them home, peel them and cut them in half. Put them in resealable bags and freeze them for quick and easy smoothies.

1ˢᵗ The Basic Smoothie

It is as simple as this!

▶ Throw a chopped frozen banana in a blender/food processor.

▶ Add some fresh or frozen fruit or veggies.

▶ Add some liquid.

▶ Add a boost or two.

▶ Blend.

▶ Pour into a mug, bottle, glass or mouth.

And remember, rinse out the blender and wash it as soon as you are done. Leaving this makes much more work for you later on.

Variations on a Theme

Use these suggestions to mix up your own smoothie goodness. Select a base and pick elements that will add character, smoothness and flavor. With a little imagination and experimentation, you can expand these lists.

Banana-Peach Smoothie

2 ripe bananas, sliced
2 cups frozen or fresh peaches
1 cup buttermilk*
¼ cup orange juice
2 tablespoons honey

▶ Place all ingredients in blender, process until smooth and scrape down sides. Serve immediately. Serves 2.

*TIP: To make buttermilk, mix 1 cup milk with 1 tablespoon lemon juice or vinegar and let milk stand for about 10 minutes.

SPECIAL NOTE: For the healthiest Banana-Peach Smoothie, add ¼ cup organic cream and 1 serving whey protein.

You don't see a lot of smoothie recipes with cream. The low-fat craze has duped many smart nutritionists and health professionals to blame the healthy fat in high quality dairy products for all sorts of problems. If you stick with high quality items, this is not the case. The addition of whey protein is important when you are under stress or exercising heavily.

1st Banana-Blueberry Smoothie

This is my all-time favorite smoothie recipe and although it undergoes slight modification as my lifestyle changes, the basic elements always stay the same. Eating blueberries always leaves me feeling alert and nourished. Blueberries are truly a super food.

½ cup frozen blueberries
½ orange
1 serving whey protein
½ cup coconut milk
1 frozen banana, chopped

▶ I cut the orange in half and slice off most of the skin, but not all of it. A little residual skin gives the drink a little kick. Process all ingredients in blender until smooth. Serves 1.

TIP: *I use a good quality whey protein from New Zealand prepared from cows that graze freely on grass and are not given any drugs. The healthy fat from the coconut milk combined with the whey protein helps prevent a sudden spike and a precipitous fall in your blood sugar.*

HOT TIP: *I buy a whole hoard of overripe bananas at the grocery store when they are dirt-cheap; you know, when they are 4 pounds for a dollar. I take them home, peel about 20, score the bananas with the back of my chef's knife and place them in a large, heavy duty resealable bag. This way you always have them available and can break off perfect chunks each time you make a smoothie!*

Banana-Mango Smoothie

1 cup peeled, cubed ripe mango
1 ripe banana, sliced
⅔ cup milk
1 teaspoon honey
¼ teaspoon vanilla

▶ Arrange mango cubes in single layer on baking sheet and freeze for about 1 hour or until firm.

▶ Combine frozen mango, banana, milk, honey and vanilla and pour into blender. Process until smooth. Serves 1.

Fruit Smoothie

2 cups apple juice
1 cup frozen strawberries and raspberries, thawed
1 large banana, sliced
1 - 2 cups raspberry yogurt

▶ Combine apple juice, strawberries and raspberries, and banana in blender.

▶ Process for just 1 minute, then add yogurt and process until they blend well. Serve immediately over ice or blend with ice. Serves 2.

Strawberry Smoothie

1 banana, peeled, sliced
1 pint fresh strawberries, quartered
1 (8 ounce) carton plain yogurt
¼ cup orange juice, optional

▶ Place all ingredients in blender. Process until smooth. Serves 2 to 3.

TIP: Our recommendation for yogurt is plain, organic, whole milk yogurt. Fruit juice may cause blood sugar swings for some people. If you need more substance in your meal, add protein particularly if you are under stress, exercising heavily or if you generally do better with protein.

 # Coco-Nut-Love

1 frozen banana, chopped
½ cup chopped walnuts
½ - 1 cup coconut milk
1 tablespoon cocoa powder
½ teaspoon vanilla

▶ Blend on high and enjoy as a dessert! Serves 1 to 2.

Strawberry-Spinach (for real) Smoothie

The first time my wife made this for me, I was skeptical, but now I am a believer.

1 frozen banana, cut into pieces
1 cup frozen spinach, drained
1 cup fresh or frozen strawberries
1 cup yogurt
2 tablespoons honey
Water to blend

▶ Blend on high and enjoy. Serves 1 to 2.

Tropical Fruit Smoothie

2 (8 ounce) cartons plain yogurt
1 cup fresh or frozen papaya
1 cup fresh or frozen mango
1 (8 ounce) can pineapple chunks, drained
1 teaspoon vanilla extract

▶ Process all ingredients in blender until smooth. Serves 4.

TIP: *We recommend using 16 ounces plain whole milk organic yogurt instead of plain yogurt for a healthier drink. Also, an optional addition is a dash of allspice.*

Peanut Power

1 banana, cut up
½ cup frozen orange juice concentrate, thawed
¼ cup peanut butter
¼ cup milk or organic whole milk

▶ Combine all ingredients in blender. Cover and blend until smooth. Add 1 cup ice cubes and blend. Serves 1.

TIP: *Add 1 serving whey protein when you are stressed out or exercising heavily.*

Very Berry Smoothie

1 cup apple juice
1 cup frozen strawberries, blackberries and raspberries, thawed
1 large banana, sliced
1 - 2 cups plain yogurt
1 tablespoon all fruit raspberry preserves, optional

▶ Combine apple juice, berries and banana in blender. Add preserves, if you like.

▶ Process for just 1 minute, then add yogurt and process until they blend well. Serve immediately over ice or blend with ice. Serves 2.

TIP: *Plain organic whole milk yogurt instead of yogurt is the healthiest choice you can make for this drink.*

For an extra boost in your smoothies, try protein powder (whey, soy, rice), flax seed/oil, powdered green drink (spirulina, wheat grass, barley grass, chlorella), cacao, goji berries, bee pollen, aerial powder or ginseng.

A Word on Cereal and Granola

Cereals, including whole grain cereals are a great quick breakfast, but they are also a processed grain and as such generally act like sugar in your body. Surprisingly, puffed whole grain brown rice cereal has a glycemic index close to that of white sugar because the exploded grain has a much larger surface area and it is therefore digested and metabolized quickly. I think cereal is a great choice for some of your breakfasts and here are a few of my recommendations:

- Food for Life Ezekiel 4:9® Sprouted Grain Cereal is one of the best.

- Muesli is made of raw oats, seeds, nuts and dried fruit.

- Grape-Nuts® has a low glycemic index, but too much can deliver a high glycemic load. Malted barley used in Grape-Nuts® is a sweetener.

- Shredded wheat is just wheat with no added sugar.

- Cheerios® is not a bad choice, but the same rule applies. Too much brings a high glycemic load, which can contribute to blood sugar issues. Bummer.

- Granola is another popular "health food", but it usually contains a ton of sugar and sometimes includes low quality oils. It can also be hard to digest. A great way to eat granola is to add it to some oatmeal near the end of cooking or pour boiling water over it in your bowl. This softens the granola and makes it easier to digest. Look for granola sweetened with honey, molasses, maple syrup or rice syrup.

Cereal

Hot Cereal

As I mentioned in the beginning, as often as possible I offer recipes that are easy to prepare and vary. Here is a great one. I start off with steel cut "Irish oats" and rotate in other whole grains with the same basic cooking instructions. Here I have included some of my favorite combinations.

1st Basic Oats

I like steel cut "Irish" oatmeal because it has a sweeter, nuttier flavor. I also like the texture and I feel they sustain me longer when I eat them. Here is what you will need:

1 cup oats
1 tablespoon whey or yogurt
1 glass bowl
1 pot

▶ Mix oats, 3 cups water and whey/yogurt in glass bowl before you go to bed and let them sit overnight. It's so easy.

▶ The next morning, dump the whole bowl of cultured goodness into a pot with additional 1 cup water and bring to a boil. Reduce heat to low-warm, put a lid on it and set a timer for 30 minutes. You'll have enough time to go take a shower, get dressed and then come back to your breakfast. It is important to cook this right — between low and warm on your stove so that it does not stick to the pot. Serves 1.

This is so easy! *You just dump things in a bowl, let it sit, then dump them into a pot and turn it on. The one step that takes the most time is waiting for the pot to boil! With a timer, you are free to go do other things. (Just make sure to clean the pot right away when you are done; oats get stubborn!)*

Breakfast-Ready Oatmeal

1½ cups quick-cooking oats
3½ cups milk
½ cup chopped pecans
Maple syrup, agave or honey to taste

▶ Combine and cook oats, milk, pecans, honey and a dash of salt in saucepan over medium heat.

▶ Bring to a boil, lower heat and simmer for 6 minutes, stirring occasionally. Let stand for several minutes before serving. Serves 1 to 2.

Cherry-Pecan Oatmeal

2 cups cooked oats, warm
½ cup dried cherries, chopped
¼ cup maple syrup, honey or agave nectar
2 tablespoons butter, softened
½ teaspoon ground cinnamon
½ cup chopped toasted pecans

▶ Combine cherries, maple syrup, butter and cinnamon in bowl. Stir into cooked oatmeal.

▶ Sprinkle toasted pecans over top of each serving. Serves 1 to 2.

TIP: *Toasting bring out the flavors of nuts and seeds. Place nuts or seeds on baking sheet and bake at 225° for 10 minutes. Be careful not to burn them.*

Some great quick breakfasts in the morning include an apple and a bag of raw or roasted almonds; a couple of celery sticks, carrots and a bag of cashews; quick oats with raisins and sunflower seeds; a cup of yogurt and some trail mix; toast with peanut butter and jelly and green tea.

Another Twist on Hot Cereal

A great option for breakfast is to make a rice cereal out of any leftover brown rice.

▶ Add leftover rice to half as much water (1 cup cooked brown rice to ½ cup water). Simmer on low for 10 to 15 minutes. Stir occasionally.

▶ Add some cinnamon, raisins and a touch of maple syrup. Serves 1.

TIP: *For a creamier cereal, use milk instead of water.*

Homemade Instant Oatmeal

Now, I know that I have just written about the benefits of grains in their whole form and the way to soak them overnight which reduces phytic acid and all of that is great. But, what about the mornings where you want something hot and satisfying, but you only have five minutes and you slacked on preparing the grains overnight.

You see, you can buy this for about eight times what it costs you to make it ahead of time. So, get yourself a mess of bulk oatmeal (about 2 pounds) and run it through your food processor with a little salt, some whey protein and a little cinnamon if you so desire. Fruit only really works if it is freeze dried, since chewy dried fruit will stick everything together and increase the potential of spoilage.

Take the finished product and put it in plastic snack or sandwich bags (depending on how much you want to eat at a time) and store them in the freezer. For about the cost of one box of a dozen little packets of instant oatmeal, you can have 80 servings of your homemade oatmeal. That really is Healthy, Fast and Cheap™!

Basic Baked Grits

2 cups quick-cooking grits
2 cups milk
¾ cup (1½ sticks) butter
4 eggs, beaten

▶ Preheat oven to 350°.

▶ Stir grits and 4 cups water in large saucepan over medium heat for about 5 minutes.

▶ Add milk and butter, cover and cook for additional 10 minutes. Remove from heat and add eggs. Pour in sprayed baking dish and bake for 30 minutes. Serves 2 to 4.

Green Chile Grits

This is one of the best ways to eat grits.

1½ cups quick-cooking grits
¾ cup (1½ sticks) butter
1 (16 ounce) package shredded cheddar cheese
½ teaspoon sea salt
1 (4 ounce) can chopped green chilies
3 eggs, beaten

▶ Preheat oven to 350°.

▶ Cook grits in 6 cups boiling water in large saucepan, stirring occasionally, until grits thicken.

▶ Stir in butter, cheese, salt, ½ teaspoon pepper and green chilies. Continue to stir and cook on low heat until butter and cheese melt.

▶ Remove from heat and fold in beaten eggs. Pour into sprayed 9 x 13-inch baking dish. Bake for 1 hour. Serves 6 to 8.

Breakfast is the most important meal of the day because it sets your metabolism in motion. You need quick, high-energy foods to sustain you. Fruit and yogurt, whole grain hot cereal, eggs, and high protein drinks are all great.

Ranch Sausage and Grits

1 cup quick-cooking grits
1 pound pork sausage, cooked, drained
1 onion, chopped, cooked
1 cup salsa
1 (8 ounce) package shredded cheddar cheese, divided

▶ Preheat oven to 350°.

▶ Cook grits according to package directions. Combine grits, sausage, onion, salsa and half cheese in bowl. Spoon into buttered 2-quart baking dish.

▶ Bake for 15 minutes. Remove from oven and add remaining cheese on top of casserole. Bake for additional 10 minutes and serve hot. Serves 6 to 8.

TIP: *Look for high quality sausage from a company like Organic Valley®, Beeler's, Diamond Organics, and regional and local manufacturers.*

 # Grits and Cheese

This is a nice change of pace from oatmeal. The flavor is savory rather than sweet and this is beneficial for sustaining energy.

1 cup grits
1 tablespoon yogurt
¼ cup shredded cheese

▶ Soak grits in 3 cups water.

▶ Cook grits according to package directions. Stir grits when you bring them to a boil and as they cool down to simmer. It is helpful to stir often while simmering, but it's not essential. They'll cook in just 20 minutes, but will get creamier the longer they cook.

▶ When done, add shredded cheese and season with a little salt and pepper. Serves 2 to 3.

Rolled Rye with Raisins and Cinnamon

1 cup rye flakes
1 tablespoon yogurt
1 (2 ounce) box raisins

▶ Soak rolled rye flakes overnight with yogurt.

▶ Add rye to 3 cups water in pot and bring to a low boil. Reduce heat to low, add raisins and cook covered for about 10 to 15 minutes. (Be sure to set your timer.) Serves 1.

TIP: These are great served with your favorite milk. For more variations on this healthy breakfast, visit my Web site at www.healthyfastandcheap.com.

Studies have shown that cinnamon may help lower blood sugar levels. Cinnamon off the spice rack should not be taken in quantity on an everyday basis because it often has naturally occurring coumarin which can cause liver toxicity and interact with blood thinning medications. Try putting ¼ or ½ teaspoon in a paper coffee filter and pouring a cup of hot water over it. This removes the coumarin and leaves the active ingredient in the water. Or try capsules of water-soluable cinnamon.

Eggs

There could be an entire chapter devoted just to the egg. This food is the saving grace for the diet of any new cook. Ready in minutes and packed with essential body-building nutrients, the egg stands alone as the most versatile and important food in many kitchens.

NOTE: For years the egg has gotten a bad rap due to the fat/cholesterol hype, but this is unwarranted. The fact is that fat and cholesterol are manufactured in the body and most often are linked with a high-refined carbohydrate diet. The best advice on fat is to focus on quality and quantity, but with an emphasis on quality.

Eggs from free-roaming chickens are significantly different from eggs from caged chickens. For example, the essential fatty acid (EFA) profile of eggs from free-roaming chickens is a nearly perfect ratio for most bodies.

Eggs from factory farms contain an average ratio of 16 omega-6 EFAs to 1 omega-3 EFA's. Our diet has an excess of omega-6 fatty acids, which among other things, leads to excessive inflammation in the body. Omega-6 fatty acids are the building blocks for pro-inflammatory compounds.

So, if you can afford them, buy the best quality, free-range, organic eggs that are available. And, ideally, get them locally whenever possible. If your budget doesn't allow you to purchase all organic products, make sure you don't compromise with animal products.

A top quality egg is dramatically different to the factory-farmed, mass-produced version. Animal fats are at the top of the food chain and serve as a repository for all the good and bad stuff lower down. All this accumulation — whether it is toxic or nutritive — ends up in your belly!

1st A Basic Healthy Breakfast

½ red onion, chopped
1 cup drained, thawed frozen spinach*
Olive oil
2 - 3 eggs

▶ Heat pot or skillet over medium heat and toss in onion, spinach and a little olive oil. (You don't need to measure out 1 cup; just throw in a bunch and add more or less next time based on how you like it.) Allow this to simmer for 2 minutes.

▶ Meanwhile, crack eggs and mix with fork or whisk. Add a little salt and pepper to eggs and mix a few more times.

▶ Add a little salt and pepper to veggies and when they cook through, about 5 minutes on medium-high heat, add eggs. Scramble as necessary. Serves 1.

TIP: *The great thing about this recipe is that it is so easy to modify to suite your taste. Just use different veggies and spices each time you make it. For example, throw in some salsa or other sauces to mix it up further! And using frozen spinach makes this meal so simple to prepare.*

*TIP: *Squeeze spinach between paper towels to completely remove excess moisture.*

Pastry and coffee is the worst meal to have at any time, especially for breakfast. The rapid assimilation of sugars into the bloodstream gives the brain an uptake of feel-good chemicals. Pastry is a high glycemic load food that leads to a blood sugar surge, storage as fat and then a crash.

 The Omelet

The omelet can be fast, but preparation is an acquired skill. I include it here so that you can impress your friends or, more importantly, your partner.

½ **cup chopped red onion**
½ **cup chopped red bell pepper**
½ **cup chopped zucchini**
Olive oil
Coriander
4 eggs

▶ Saute veggies with splash of olive or coconut oil, dash of coriander and salt.

▶ Crack 2 eggs into bowl while veggies cook and beat the heck out of them with a whisk. (A fork won't cut it for an omelet. The whisk whips up more air for a fluffier omelet.)

▶ Clean up what you can because you have 1 minute or 2 to wait for the veggies to get nice and sweet. After 2 minutes, take veggies out of pan and place on a plate.

▶ Pour some more oil in pan, swirl it around to cover the whole surface and add enough egg mixture to evenly cover the entire base of the pan. Let the egg layer cook until bubbles begin to rise to the surface.

▶ When the egg firms up most of the way, but is still a little runny, add half the veggies to one side of the pan and flip the other side of the omelet over onto it.

▶ Let the omelet cook for additional 2 minutes. Slide a large flipping spatula underneath the omelet and carefully lift it from the pan. You can repeat the above steps with the remaining eggs and veggies as needed. Serves 2.

Omelets are great for breakfast or late-night meals. Check out chopped vegetables in the frozen food section to use in the center of the omelet. It will save on chopping time.

Bacon-Cheese Omelet

2 strips bacon
2 green onions with tops, chopped
2 eggs
1 tablespoon milk
1 tablespoon butter
½ cup shredded cheddar cheese

▶ Fry bacon crispy in skillet, drain, cool and crumble. Save a little of the bacon drippings and saute onion until it is translucent.

▶ Beat eggs with milk in bowl. Heat butter in omelet pan over medium heat and pour in egg mixture. Tilt pan or use spoon to move liquid of eggs around pan to cook evenly. Cook until eggs are almost firm in center.

▶ Sprinkle bacon, onions and cheese evenly over half of eggs. Fold one half of omelet over to cover cheese and continue cooking for 1 to 2 minutes until cheese melts. Serve immediately. Serves 1.

Western Omelet

4 eggs
¼ cup milk
Butter
⅓ cup shredded cheddar cheese
⅓ cup cooked, diced ham
¼ cup finely chopped onion
**¼ cup finely chopped green peppers or chopped
        green chilies, drained**
¼ cup chopped tomatoes
Salsa

▶ Beat eggs with milk in bowl. Melt butter in omelet pan or skillet over medium heat and pour eggs into pan. Tilt pan or use spoon to move liquid of eggs around pan to cook evenly. Cook until eggs are almost firm in the middle.

▶ Sprinkle cheese, ham, onion, green peppers and tomatoes over half of the eggs. Fold other half of omelet over top to cover cheese mixture and continue cooking for additional 1 or 2 minutes or until eggs are firm and cheese melts. Slide out of pan, pour salsa over top and serve immediately. Serves 2.

Bacon and Egg Burrito

2 eggs, scrambled
Olive oil
2 slices bacon or Canadian bacon, cooked, chopped
¼ cup shredded cheddar cheese
1 whole grain or flour tortilla

▶ Beat eggs in bowl with fork or whisk. Cook in oiled skillet and stir eggs frequently until they are firm.

▶ Sprinkle eggs, bacon and cheese in middle of tortilla. Fold tortilla sides over and place seam-side down on dinner plate.

▶ Microwave for 30 seconds or just until mixture heats thoroughly. Serves 1.

TIP: Here is the deal with bacon. If you use high quality animal products like hogs that have been raised as omnivores, eating a variety of foods (including grubs), rooting around, living with access to sunlight without antibiotics or vermicide, the fat is, contrary to politically correct nutrition, really good for a lot of people. Unfortunately for you and me, it is still really hard to get good quality animal products across the country.

Sunrise Tacos

4 eggs, cooked, scrambled
Olive oil
½ cup shredded cheddar cheese, divided
½ cup salsa, divided
2 whole wheat, sprouted grain or flour tortillas

▶ Beat eggs in bowl with fork or whisk. Cook in oiled skillet and stir frequently until they are firm.

▶ For each taco, spread half scrambled eggs, ¼ cup cheese and ¼ cup salsa on tortilla and roll. Serves 2.

TIP: It is always better to use whole wheat or sprouted grain tortillas instead of flour or corn tortillas. If you cannot find whole wheat or sprouted grain, flour will be fine.

Breakfast Tacos

4 eggs
4 flour or whole wheat flour tortillas
1 cup cooked, chopped ham, turkey, beef or buffalo
1 cup shredded cheddar cheese

▶ Beat eggs in bowl with fork or whisk. Cook in sprayed skillet and stir frequently until they are firm. Lay tortillas flat and spoon eggs over 4 tortillas. Sprinkle with ham and cheese.

▶ Place tacos in oven-safe dish and broil for 1 minute or until cheese melts. Immediately remove and roll up or fold into halves. Serve immediately. Serves 2.

Quesadilla Pie

Butter
1 (4 ounce) can chopped green chilies, drained
½ pound ground turkey or pork sausage, cooked
1 (16 ounce) package shredded cheddar cheese
3 eggs, well beaten
1½ cups milk
¾ cup biscuit mix
Hot salsa

▶ Preheat oven to 350°.

▶ Butter 9-inch pie pan. Sprinkle green chilies, cooked sausage and cheddar cheese in pie pan.

▶ In separate bowl, combine eggs, milk and biscuit mix. Pour mixture over green chilies, sausage and cheese and bake for 30 to 40 minutes. Serve with salsa on top of each slice. Serves 2 to 3.

TIP: *Our recommendation is Bob's Red Mill® or Arrowhead Mills Whole Wheat biscuit mix.*

The best cereals for breakfast include muesli, Grape-Nuts®, Cheerios® and Food for Life Ezekiel 4:9® Sprouted Grain cereal.

English Muffin Breakfast Sandwich

Save yourself a bunch of dough and make these at home with better quality ingredients. Make four at once and bake them when you are ready to eat them.

4 - 6 eggs
1 (16 ounce) package precooked Canadian bacon slices, halved
1 (12 ounce) package 4 whole wheat or sprouted grain English
       muffins, halved, toasted
4 slices cheddar cheese

▶ Preheat oven to 325°.

▶ Lightly scramble eggs in skillet over medium heat and stir often. Season according to taste.

▶ Heat bacon in pan alongside eggs near the end of cooking.

▶ Spoon egg mixture onto bottom of muffin, add cheese slice, bacon and muffin top.

▶ Place on baking sheet and bake for about 10 minutes or just until cheese begins to melt. Yields 4 sandwiches.

If you can afford them, buy the best free-range, organic eggs available. The essential fatty acid profile of eggs from free-roaming chickens is a nearly perfect ratio for most bodies. Too much of omega fatty acids in eggs from caged chickens can cause inflammation in the body.

Waffles, Pancakes & French Toast

French Toast

2 eggs
1 cup milk
1 teaspoon sugar or maple syrup
1 teaspoon vanilla
1 tablespoon butter
6 - 8 slices white bread
Honey or maple syrup

▶ Beat eggs, milk, sugar or maple syrup, and vanilla in medium bowl. Spread butter on griddle and heat until it melts.

▶ Dip both sides of bread into milk-egg mixture. Cook on both sides until brown.

▶ Remove from griddle and drizzle honey or maple syrup. Serves 3 to 4.

Quick, Light, Crispy Waffles

The secret to this quick recipe is not the surprise club soda addition, but getting a really good waffle iron!

2 cups biscuit mix
1 egg
½ cup melted butter
1⅓ cups club soda

▶ Preheat waffle iron.

▶ Combine all ingredients in bowl and stir with spoon. Pour just enough batter to cover waffle iron and cook. Yields 6 to 8 waffles.

TIP: To have waffles for a "company weekend", make them before the guests arrive. Freeze the waffles separately on a baking sheet and place in large plastic bags. To reheat, bake at 350° for about 10 minutes.

Basic Pancakes

2 cups flour or whole wheat flour*
1 teaspoon sugar
1 tablespoon baking powder
2 eggs
1½ - 2 cups milk, divided
Butter or coconut oil
Maple syrup
½ cup melted butter

▶ Combine flour, sugar, baking powder and ¼ teaspoon salt in large bowl.

▶ In separate bowl, beat eggs and 1½ cups milk. Pour egg mixture into flour mixture and stir until smooth. If batter is too thick, add a little milk.

▶ Heat griddle and coat lightly with butter or oil. Slowly pour circle of batter on griddle to equal desired size of pancake. After bubbles form on top and edges brown, gently flip pancake to cook on other side.

▶ Serve immediately with warm syrup and melted butter. Yields 10 to 12 medium pancakes.

*TIP: *Experiment with healthy flours by adding small amounts of other whole grain flours like oat flour, brown rice flour, spelt flour, buckwheat flour, etc. In fact, many food processors can grind whole grains into flour at home, which not only saves you money but is the healthiest way to eat it!*

> *Just like the hot cereal recipes, when I make pancakes, I mix the ingredients in a bowl (except the baking powder) then let it set overnight in the refrigerator, which reduces phytic acid and makes it easier to digest and does not deplete minerals in digestion. Then in the morning, I toss in my baking powder (non-aluminum based), mix and fry. Pretty easy when you get in the habit of it.*

Breads

Study-Group Coffee Cake

1 (16 ounce) package blueberry muffin mix with blueberries or
        whole grain muffin mix
⅓ cup sour cream
1 egg
½ cup honey

▶ Preheat oven to 400°.

▶ Stir muffin mix, sour cream, egg and ½ cup water in bowl until it
is just barely combined. Rinse blueberries, add to batter and fold
in two or three times. Do not over mix.

▶ Pour into sprayed 7 x 11-inch baking dish. Bake for about
25 minutes and cool.

▶ Drizzle honey over coffee cake. Serves 4.

TIP: *If you use whole grain muffin mix, add 1 cup frozen blueberries,
thawed, before baking.*

Quick and Crunchy Breadsticks

1 (8 count) package hot dog buns
1 cup (2 sticks) butter
Garlic powder
Paprika

▶ Preheat oven to 225°.

▶ Take each half bun and slice in half lengthwise. Butter all
breadsticks and sprinkle each lightly with garlic powder
and paprika.

▶ Place on baking sheet and bake for 45 minutes. Serves 6 to 8.

TIP: *The best hot dog buns to use are whole grain or sprouted grain
buns or rolls.*

Banana-Nut Bread

½ cup (1 stick) butter
1 cup sugar
2 eggs
2 cups flour
1 teaspoon baking soda
1 teaspoon ground cinnamon
4 ripe bananas
1 cup chopped pecans

▶ Preheat oven to 350°.

▶ Cream butter and sugar in bowl and add eggs one at a time. Stir vigorously.

▶ In separate bowl, combine flour, baking soda and cinnamon and stir into butter mixture a little at a time. Mash bananas and add to mixture. Stir well and add nuts.

▶ Pour into sprayed loaf pan and bake for 50 to 60 minutes. Yields about 8 to 10 slices.

TIP: *The recommended substitutions for healthier ingredients include unrefined sugar and whole wheat pastry flour.*

Mozzarella Loaf

1 (16 ounce) loaf French bread
¼ cup grated parmesan cheese
6 tablespoons (¾ stick) butter, softened
½ teaspoon garlic salt
12 slices mozzarella cheese

▶ Preheat oven to 375°.

▶ Cut loaf into 1-inch thick slices. Combine parmesan cheese, butter and garlic salt in bowl and spread mixture on each slice of bread.

▶ Place mozzarella slices between bread slices. Reshape loaf, press firmly together and brush remaining butter mixture on outside of loaf. Bake for 8 to 10 minutes. Serves 6 to 8.

TIP: *Use whole grain French bread if you can find it.*

1st Healthy, Fast and Cheap™ Cornbread

1 cup yogurt, room temperature
¼ cup butter, softened
3 tablespoons maple syrup or honey
⅔ cup whole kernel frozen corn, thawed
⅔ cup whole wheat flour
2 eggs, beaten
2 teaspoons baking powder

▶ Pour all ingredients except eggs and baking powder into blender and away you go. Zoom, zoom, zoom. Give it a good 5 minutes to beat the heck out of the batter so everything is ground up into a true batter. Now, for the really easy part. Keep the cover on and let stand for 8 hours in refrigerator.

▶ When you are ready to bake, preheat oven to 350°.

▶ Just add eggs, baking powder and 1 teaspoon salt to batter mixture and mix well.

▶ Pour batter immediately into sprayed baking pan. Bake for about 30 minutes or until it begins to pull away from sides. Serves 6 to 8.

Fast Cheddar Cornbread

This isn't the healthiest version of cheddar cornbread, but it's the quickest and is almost a meal in itself.

2 (8.5 ounce) packages cornbread muffin mix
2 eggs, beaten
½ cup milk
½ cup plain yogurt
1 (14 ounce) can cream-style corn
½ cup shredded cheddar cheese

▶ Preheat oven to 400°.

▶ Mix cornbread mix, eggs, milk and yogurt in bowl until they blend well.

▶ Stir in corn and cheese and pour into sprayed 9 x 13-inch baking dish. Bake for 18 to 20 minutes or until light brown. Serves 6 to 8.

Cheddar Cornbread

Healthy, Fast and Cheap™ Cornbread recipe (page 103)
⅔ cup shredded cheddar cheese

▶ Make Healthy, Fast and Cheap™ Cornbread recipe on page 103. When you add eggs, add cheddar cheese. Bake according to recipe. Serves 6 to 8.

Pesto Poppers

1 (11 ounce) package refrigerated breadsticks
¼ cup (½ stick) butter, melted
2 tablespoons prepared pesto
¼ teaspoon garlic powder
3 tablespoons grated parmesan cheese

▶ Preheat oven to 375°.

▶ Place breadsticks on baking pan. Combine melted butter, pesto and garlic powder in bowl and brush over bread strips.

▶ Sprinkle with parmesan cheese. Bake for about 12 minutes or until golden brown. Serves 4 to 6.

TIP: The recommended bread to use is whole grain or sprouted grain.

Ranch-Style French Bread

1 (16 ounce) loaf French bread
½ cup (1 stick) butter, softened
1 teaspoon garlic powder
1 teaspoon dried chives or onion flakes
2 tablespoons shredded parmesan cheese

▶ Preheat oven to 350°.

▶ Cut loaf in half horizontally. Mix butter, garlic powder, chives and cheese in bowl.

▶ Spread butter mixture on bread. Wrap bread in foil. Bake for 15 minutes. Serves 6 to 8.

TIP: Use whole wheat French bread if you can find it.

Move On

Basic Foods
for the Microwave
Sandwiches & Wraps
Salads
Salad Meals
Salad Dressings
Beans and Bean Soups
Chicken Soups
Veggie Soups
Hearty Soups
Pizzas

Leaving Home Cookbook
and Survival Guide

Move On Contents

Move On Contents

Lunch

You probably need options that are not only quick, but also portable. In most cases how you transport lunch is tied to what you can have for lunch. I have included a guide to food court/restaurant eating as well on pages 33-35 (Options When Eating Out). Lunch is an essential part of your Healthy, Fast and Cheap™ plan so you need to have options.

Basic Foods for the Microwave

Times may vary slightly from one microwave to another.

Easy Scrambled Eggs

1 tablespoon butter
2 eggs, beaten
2 tablespoons milk
3 tablespoons shredded cheddar cheese
Salsa

▶ Put butter in microwave-safe bowl, cover with plastic wrap (make small vent) and microwave on HIGH for 15 seconds. Add eggs, milk and cheese and mix with fork. Cover with plastic wrap (make small vent) and microwave for about 30 seconds or until eggs are almost firm, but still slightly moist. Let eggs rest for another 1 to 2 minutes (they continue to cook) and serve with salsa. Serves 1.

TIP: *You can roll eggs in whole wheat or flour tortilla and eat it walking out the door. To heat tortillas, put several drops water on paper towel and wrap tortilla inside. Microwave on HIGH for about 20 seconds.*

Fruity Oatmeal

1⅓ cups oats
2 teaspoons sugar
2 teaspoons ground cinnamon
1 peeled, cored, chopped apple
1 - 2 tablespoons raisins
1 tablespoon chopped pecans, walnuts or almonds
1 cup milk

▶ Combine all ingredients, except milk, in microwave-safe bowl, cover with paper towel and microwave on HIGH for 1 minute. Stir, rotate bowl and microwave for additional 1 minute. Pour milk over top and eat. Serves 1 to 2.

Apple-Cheese Roll-Ups

4 delicious apples
1 cup shredded cheddar cheese
4 large whole wheat or flour tortillas

▶ Core and chop or dice apples. Spread apples and cheese evenly among 4 tortillas and roll or fold in half. Microwave on HIGH for about 15 to 20 seconds or until cheese melts. Serves 2 to 4.

Basic Baked Potato

1 medium baking potato or sweet potato
1 paper towel

▶ Poke holes in potato several times with fork so it will not explode. Wrap in paper towel and microwave on HIGH for 1 minute 30 seconds. Remove potato, turn over and rotate. (If you have microwave with revolving plate inside, this step is not necessary.)

▶ Microwave for additional 1 minute 30 seconds. Remove from microwave and squeeze sides. If it is soft, it is ready. If it is hard, cook for additional 30 seconds or until done. Potato continues to cook after you remove it from microwave. Serves 1.

TIP: *Sweet potatoes have many more nutrients than baking potatoes and are by far, the better choice of foods.*

Chili-Cheese Baked Potato

1 baking potato
1 (5 ounce) can chili
Shredded cheddar cheese

▶ Use the instructions shown on page 109 for microwaving Basic Baked Potato. Open can of chili and put contents into microwave-safe bowl. Cover with wax paper or plastic wrap (leave small vent) and microwave on HIGH for 1 minute. Stir and rotate bowl. Microwave for additional 1 minute or until chili is thoroughly hot. Pour over mashed up baked potato and top with cheese. Serves 1.

TIP: *For a variation, open 1 (10 ounce) can cream of broccoli soup and pour into microwave-safe bowl. Microwave on HIGH for 1 minute, stir and rotate bowl. Microwave for additional 1 minute or until thoroughly hot. Stir well and pour over mashed up baked potato and top with cheese.*

Fast Fish Filet

2 (¼ pound) fish filets
2 tablespoons teriyaki sauce

▶ Place filets on microwave-safe plate and sprinkle with teriyaki sauce. Cover with plastic wrap and make small vent in plastic wrap. Microwave on HIGH for about 1 minute 30 seconds, rotate plate and cook additional 2 minutes.

▶ Use fork to see if fish flakes, is opaque color throughout and is done. If needed, cook for additional 30 seconds until fish flakes. Serves 1.

Easy Baked Beans

1 (15 ounce) can pork and beans
1 tablespoon ketchup
1 tablespoon molasses or honey
¼ teaspoon onion powder

▶ Mix all ingredients in microwave-safe bowl and cover with wax paper or paper towel. Microwave on HIGH for about 1 minute and stir. Rotate position in microwave. Microwave for additional 2 minutes or until thoroughly hot. Serves 2.

Simple Salmon Steak

1 (1½ pound) salmon steak
Garlic powder or garlic salt
Lemon juice

► Sprinkle garlic powder and lemon juice over both sides of steak and place on microwave-safe plate. Cover plate with wax paper or plastic wrap. Microwave on HIGH for 2 minutes, rotate plate and cook additional 1 minute. Look inside salmon to see if it is light pink. If it is not light pink, cook for additional 15 seconds or until done. Do not overcook. It will dry out fish. Serves 3 to 4.

Steamed Corn-on-the-Cob

4 ears corn-on-the-cob

► Place corn in microwave-safe dish, add ¼ cup water and cover with lid or plastic wrap. If you use plastic wrap, leave small vent for steam to escape. Microwave on HIGH for 2 to 3 minutes or until done. Use butter, salt and pepper to season. Serves 4.

Steamed Broccoli

2 cups broccoli florets

► Place broccoli in microwave-safe dish, add ¼ cup water and cover with lid or plastic wrap. If you use plastic wrap, leave small vent for steam to escape. Microwave on HIGH for 60 to 90 seconds or until done. Use butter, salt and pepper to season. Serves 2.

Steamed Green Beans

2 cups fresh green beans

► Pinch ends off green beans and cut into 2-inch pieces. Place beans in microwave-safe dish, add ⅓ cup water and cover with lid or plastic wrap. If you use plastic wrap, leave small vent for steam to escape. Microwave on HIGH for 2 to 3 minutes or until done. Use butter, salt and pepper to season. Serves 2.

Sandwiches & Wraps

1st The Sandwich

A holy and beautiful thing!

The potential for innovations in sandwich preparation is huge! Preparing several sandwich options before the week starts can help you enjoy Healthy, Fast and Cheap™ lunches several days a week without it becoming monotonous. Here are some star players on the sandwich team.

Breads

Choose sprouted grain when available. My favorite is Food for Life sprouted grain breads, but there are many other varieties. I like to toast this to bring out the flavor.

- Food for Life Genesis 1:29® bread is very hearty.

- Food for Life Ezekiel 4:9® bread is my standby, especially Ezekiel 4:9® Raisin Bread. This is so good!

- Bakery breads that are fresh and made with high quality flour, water, oil and salt are much better than the stuff sitting on the shelves at the grocery. Whole grain bread made with freshly ground grain is the best option.

- Food for Life also makes amazing sprouted grain tortillas for wraps.

- Sprouted grain breads do not use any flour. The sprouting process makes all the ingredients more readily digestible and nutritious. Food for Life breads go from sprouting to a mash. This is made into a batter then baked. The result is a super high quality bread.

Spreads

- Spicy mustard

- Mayonnaise

- Miso Mayo — Take 2 parts mayonnaise, 1 part miso and dash of black pepper. Stir well and pour into airtight container.

- Herbed Cream Cheese — Blend one package organic cream cheese with a dash of pepper, basil, oregano and ¼ cup chopped scallions. Blend ingredients in food processor or with spoon in bowl.

- Hummus — Take 2 cups cooked garbanzo beans (chick-peas), along with a bit of water from the beans, 2 heaping tablespoons tahini, garlic clove and a little salt. This is best done in a food processor. Top with a sprinkle of paprika. Garbanzo beans can be purchased in the can, ready to go or you can cook them yourself at home. (See cooking beans on page 157.)

- Tahini-Miso Mustard — Take 3 parts raw or roasted sesame tahini, one part miso and one part spicy mustard. Mix these in a small bowl and use on bread or toast for a zesty and satisfying spread.

Cheese

Go organic and pasture-fed when possible; the extra cost is worth it.

- Provolone
- Mozzarella
- Havarti
- Swiss
- Cheddar
- Monterey Jack
- Colby
- Colby Jack

Miso is a cultured bean paste traditionally made from soybeans, it's also available made from chick-peas, barley and rice. It's a great source of beneficial enzymes and protein with a savory rich flavor.

Meats

Always choose the minimally processed, highest quality meats available and there are a wealth of lunch meats to pick from.

- Turkey (smoked, roasted)
- Roast beef
- Chicken (smoked, roasted, Cajun)
- Pastrami
- Ham

Fish

- Classic tuna salad is made from mayo, celery and spring onions, but you can add capers, black pepper, chopped bell pepper, mustard or other spices for a change of pace.
- Salmon is always readily available just like tuna and can be prepared in much the same way.
- Sardines, whether fresh or canned, are a nutritional powerhouse. They contain essential fatty acids, protein and are rich in calcium. Sardines are especially wonderful with black olives, olive oil, lemon juice and hot sauce.

NOTE: You may want to have breath mints on hand after the onion and fish!

Lettuce

The combination of lettuce, tomato and salty substances is so tasty when placed on bread and there are many varieties of lettuce to choose from. The majority of lettuce eaten in America is iceberg lettuce, but I shun this option and go for more nutritionally dense counterparts.

- Red and green leaf lettuce
- Romaine
- Boston bibb
- Spring-mix (This is usually a blend of baby romaine, arugula, baby spinach, radicchio, baby chard and others.)

You can prepare your lettuce deli-style by rolling several leaves together and thin slicing across the central stem or you can simply throw a few leaves on your sandwich.

Tomato

- On the vine (my favorite choice)
- Roma (probably the best price and a good all-around option)
- Beefsteak (these are great for that full-sized sandwich slice)
- Heirloom (a catch-all name to cover many different types of tomatoes that are open-pollinated, bred and stabilized using classic breeding practices)
- Yellow and orange tomatoes (these have less acidity than the red varieties)
- Cherry or grape tomatoes

Onions

- Red (pronounced and vibrant flavor)
- White (strong flavors)
- Yellow (slightly milder than the white varieties)
- Vidalia® or Texas SuperSweet 1015 (large, mild and sweet varieties)

Sprouts

Make your sandwich a real meal with a pile of sprouts. Throw on a big handful along with some olive oil, lemon juice and a dash of salt and pepper. You're good to go!

- Alfalfa sprouts
- Radish sprouts (tangy)
- Garlic sprouts
- Sunflower sprouts

Any seed, bean, grain and most nuts can be sprouted. Sprouting turns a nugget of potential energy into a powerhouse young vegetable.

Tahini is a refined sesame seed paste. Look for whole sesame seed paste, whole sesame seed butter or for tahini that is made from whole sesame seeds.

The New American Sandwich Classic

2 slices sprouted grain bread
Tahini-Miso Mustard (see page 113)
2 slices free-range turkey
Sprouts
Olive oil
Lemon juice or vinegar
1 tomato
Lettuce

▶ Toast bread and spread on some Tahini-Miso Mustard. Place a few slices of turkey, some sprouts and a splash of olive oil, lemon juice (or vinegar), salt and pepper. Lay on tomato slices and some chopped lettuce and cap it with other slice of toast. Serves 1.

 # A Righteous Wrap

This wrap will serve you well every day of the semester or work week.

Hummus (see page 113)
Sprouts
Finely chopped onion
Lettuce
Tomatoes, sliced or chopped, drained
1 sprouted grain tortilla
Pumpkin seeds, toasted
Seasonings

▶ Spread some hummus, sprouts, finely chopped onion, lettuce and tomato on tortilla. Throw in a small handful of toasted pumpkin seeds and for extra flavor add a dash of your favorite dressing or seasoning. Serves 1.

TIP: *You can modify this basic recipe with chopped zucchini, olives, roasted veggies or with a hit of grated parmesan cheese.*

Toast-on-the-Go

Somewhere it is written in stone: Thou shall eat toast! If you are rushing around and have only 3 minutes to get out of the house, here is what to do.

2 slices bread
Tahini-Miso Mustard (see page 113)
Butter
Peanut butter
Jelly

▶ Pop 2 slices of bread or better yet, Food for Life sprouted grain bread, in the toaster. (Go and pack your bag while it cooks, if you like!) Place the toast on a paper towel and lather on Tahini-Miso Mustard, Earth Balance® spread or butter along with a sprinkling of nutritional yeast or peanut butter and jelly. Serves 1.

Homemade Egg Salad Sandwiches

4 eggs, hard-boiled
⅓ cup mayonnaise
1 tablespoon dijon-style mustard
1 rib celery, minced
Bread

▶ Mash eggs with fork in bowl and stir in mayonnaise, mustard and celery. Add a little salt and pepper. Spread on bread and serve as sandwiches. Serves 2.

TIP: *To hard boil eggs, place eggs in single layer in pan. Add water to 1 inch above eggs. Heat to a boil over medium-high heat. Cover and remove from heat. Let stand for 15 minutes for large eggs, 18 minutes for extra large eggs, 12 minutes for medium-sized eggs. Use a timer. Move pan to sink and run cold water over eggs until they are cool. Refrigerate in shell for no more than a week.*

To peel: Tap egg on hard surface and roll between your hands until shell is cracked all over Begin peeling at the large end.

Peanut Butter Burrito

2 - 3 tablespoons creamy or chunky peanut butter
1 (10 inch) whole wheat flour tortilla
1 banana, thin sliced

▶ Spread peanut butter on tortilla and place on hot skillet. When peanut butter is soft, toss on layer of thin sliced banana.

▶ Roll tortilla and fold ends under last roll. Serves 1.

TIP: *If you don't have a banana, use apple slices, peaches, strawberries and/or raisins. Throw all of them on the tortilla if you want. Make it up as you go!*

Turkey-Bacon Wraps

4 large whole wheat or sprouted grain tortillas
Mayonnaise
8 slices deli turkey
8 slices cooked Canadian bacon or ham
Lettuce, shredded
Tomatoes, chopped

▶ Top each tortilla with mayonnaise, 2 slices turkey, 2 slices Canadian bacon, lettuce and tomatoes. Fold edges over to enclose filling. Serve immediately or wrap in wax paper and refrigerate. Serves 2 to 4.

TIP: *Tahini-Miso Mustard on page 113 is a good substitute for mayonnaise. To add flavor and substance, include thin slices of red onion and/or sliced black olives.*

Buffalo-Avocado Burgers

1 (1 pound) package ground buffalo or lean ground beef
1 ripe avocado
¼ cup mayonnaise
1 tablespoon lemon juice
1 (4 ounce) can green chilies, drained
4 whole grain or sprouted grain hamburger buns

► Form meat into 4 quarter-pound burgers. Dust with pepper. Cover and cook until juice runs out the top. Flip over and repeat.

► Mash avocado with mayonnaise, lemon juice and ½ teaspoon salt with fork in bowl. Stir in green chilies.

► Place meat on buns and spread with avocado mayonnaise mixture. Serve as is or top with lettuce and sliced tomatoes. Serves 2 to 4.

Grilled Cheese Sandwiches

4 slices cheddar cheese
4 slices bread
3 tablespoons butter, softened

► Place 2 slices cheese on each of 2 slices bread.

► Top with remaining 2 slices bread. Butter outside of sandwiches.

► Brown sandwiches in large skillet over medium heat on both sides until golden brown and cheese melts. Serves 2.

TIP: The best bread to use is whole grain sourdough or sprouted grain bread.

All you need to do is eat avocado consistently for a month to see for yourself how great this food is. It contains wonderful raw, monounsaturated fat that actually helps keep the body clean and lubricated. Good, healthy fat from avocado is not only acceptable, it is essential

Grilled Open-Face Sandwich

*This is a great recipe for leftover chicken. Check out the recipe for
Roast Chicken on page 209.*

2 cups cooked, chopped chicken
½ cup drained pickle relish
2 eggs, hard-boiled, chopped
⅓ cup mayonnaise
Bread
Butter

▶ Combine chicken, pickle relish, eggs and mayonnaise in
  bowl. Toast 5 slices of favorite bread and spread butter on
  untoasted side.

▶ Spread chicken mixture on untoasted side of bread and broil until
  mixture browns lightly. Serve piping hot. Serves 3 to 4.

TIP: *Real pickles and relish are lacto-fermented, a process not unlike
     making yogurt. Lacto-fermented foods help us digest and use the
     food better. Keep an eye out for them. You can use black or green
     olives as a variation in this recipe.*

A Special Grilled Cheese Sandwich

Butter, softened
2 slices 7-grain bread
2 tablespoons chipotle mayonnaise
2 slices sharp cheddar cheese
2 tablespoons cooked, chopped smoked turkey or chicken
1 avocado, thinly sliced

▶ For each sandwich, spread softened butter on 2 thick slices of
  7-grain bread and place 1 slice, butter side down, in heavy skillet.
  Spread with 1 tablespoon of mayonnaise and one slice of cheese.

▶ Sprinkle with turkey and avocado slices. Top with second slice of
  cheese and remaining slice of bread spread with other tablespoon
  of mayonnaise. Spread butter on top of bread. Cook in skillet on
  medium-high heat for about 2 minutes until it browns.

▶ Turn sandwich over and cook for additional 2 minutes or until
  brown and cheese melts. Serves 1.

Healthy Hot Dogs

1 (1 pound) package organic turkey frankfurters
8 whole grain hot dog buns
1 (8 ounce) can sauerkraut, well drained
Caraway seeds
Homemade Thousand Island Dressing (see page 156)

▶ Preheat oven to 325°.

▶ Pierce frankfurters and place into split buns.

▶ Arrange 2 tablespoons sauerkraut over each frank and sprinkle with caraway seeds.

▶ Place in 9 x 13-inch shallow pan and drizzle with Homemade Thousand Island Dressing.

▶ Heat for 10 minutes or just until franks are thoroughly hot. Serves 6 to 8.

 # Better-Than-a-Power Bar Snack

Why buy glorified corn syrup and soy protein isolate when you can achieve better results at home for less?

Food for Life Ezekiel 4:9® raisin bread
Almond or peanut butter
Fruit preserves (no sugar added) or honey

▶ Take a few slices of bread and toast it. Spread almond or peanut butter and fruit preserves or honey on toast. Wrap it in paper towel, wax paper, sandwich bag or place it in a Tupperware® container and you are ready to go. When hunger calls, you have a high protein, nutritionally dense snack that is tasty and filling. Serves 1.

www.healthyfastandcheap.com is the ultimate Internet resource for the healthy college lifestyle.

Everyday Sloppy Joes

1 (1 pound) package buffalo or lean ground beef
1 (6 ounce can) Italian tomato paste
2 teaspoons Worcestershire sauce
6 whole grain hamburger buns, split, toasted

▶ Cook beef in skillet until brown, stir to separate meat and spoon off fat.

▶ Add 4 ounces water to tomato paste a little at a time and mix well.

▶ Add tomato paste, Worcestershire sauce, ⅛ teaspoon pepper and water as necessary. Heat thoroughly and stir often. Serve on buns. Serves 3 to 4.

Super Chicken Club

3 slices whole grain bread
Mayonnaise
1 slice sharp cheddar cheese
2 thin slices tomatoes
Small bunch bean sprouts, alfalfa sprouts or sunflower sprouts
1 boneless, skinless chicken breast half, cooked
3 lettuce leaves
2 thin slices deli ham
1 slice pepper Jack cheese

▶ Toast bread in toaster or under broiler. Spread mayonnaise on 1 slice bread and stack 1 slice cheddar cheese, tomatoes and bean sprouts on top.

▶ Spread mayonnaise on both sides of second slice of bread and lay it on top of sprouts. Stack chicken breast, lettuce, ham and pepper Jack cheese on top and cover with last slice of bread. Yields 1 sandwich.

Meatball Heroes

Any bread, roll, or bun will work for these. Look for fresh baked bread made from simple, high quality ingredients. Local bakeries and the freezer section are locations to check out.

1 (16 ounce) container marinara sauce
1 (16 ounce) package frozen bell peppers, thawed
½ onion, minced
1 (12 ounce) package cooked Italian meatballs

▶ Combine marinara sauce, bell peppers and onion in large saucepan and cook on medium heat for 5 minutes.

▶ Add meatballs, cover and gently boil for about 5 minutes or until meatballs are hot. Spoon into split club rolls and serve hot. Serves 4 to 6.

TIP: The healthiest version of this recipe calls for No-Fuss Meatballs on page 64.

Reuben Sandwich

Butter
2 slices rye bread
1 slice Swiss cheese
Generous slices corned beef or pastrami
2 tablespoons sauerkraut, drained
Dijon-style mustard

▶ Butter 1 slice bread on 1 side and place butter-side down in skillet over low heat. Layer cheese, corned beef and sauerkraut on bread.

▶ Spread mustard on 1 side of other slice, butter opposite side of bread and place butter side up on sauerkraut.

▶ Cook until bottom browns, turn carefully and brown other side. Serves 1.

TIP: Applegate Farms® pastrami and corned beef are the best on the market.

Homemade Ham or Beef Spread

This is great for leftover ham, roast or chicken.

2 cups cooked, chopped ham or roast beef
¾ cup sweet pickle relish
2 ribs celery, finely chopped
2 eggs, hard-boiled, chopped
Mayonnaise

▶ Chop meat in food processor or with knife. Add relish, celery and eggs in bowl and add a little salt and pepper.

▶ Fold in enough mayonnaise to make mixture spreadable and refrigerate.

▶ Spread on crackers or bread for sandwiches. Serves 3 to 4.

Pizza Sandwich

4 English muffins
½ - 1 pound turkey or pork sausage, cooked, drained
1½ cups pizza sauce or Italian-style tomato paste
4 ounces fresh mushrooms, chopped
1 (8 ounce) package shredded mozzarella cheese

▶ Split muffins and layer ingredients on each muffin half ending with cheese. Broil until cheese melts. Serves 4.

TIP: *I like Food for Life sprouted English muffins, but really, you can make this with any bread you have at home.*

Sprouted grain breads are easier to digest, more nutritious and maintain freshness longer than other breads. They can be found in the freezer or refrigerator section in the grocery store.

Hot Cornbread Sandwich

2 (8 ounce) packages corn muffin mix
2 eggs, beaten
⅔ cup milk
12 slices or 10 ounces favorite cheese
6 slices deli ham, turkey or chicken

▶ Preheat oven to 400°.

▶ Combine muffin mix, eggs and milk in bowl, mixing well. Pour half of mixture into sprayed 7 x 11-inch baking dish.

▶ Carefully place 6 slices of cheese, then ham slices over cheese and remaining cheese slices on top of ham. Spoon remaining cornbread batter over top of cheese.

▶ Bake for 25 minutes or until cornbread is golden brown. Cut into squares and serve hot. Serves 4 to 6.

TIP: *The healthiest way to prepare this recipe is to make Cheddar Cornbread on page 104.*

Tuna Burgers

1 (6 ounce) can tuna fish or 1 (6 ounce) can wild
    Alaskan salmon, drained
1 egg, beaten
½ cup crushed crackers
Whole grain hamburger buns

▶ Combine tuna, egg and crackers in bowl and mix well. Shape into patties.

▶ Brown patties in sprayed non-stick skillet on both sides (or fry in a little canola oil). Serve on bun with favorite accompaniments. Serves 1 to 2.

TIP: *With all of the concern about mercury in fish, you may substitute canned wild Alaskan salmon or other canned fish.*

Tuna Tortilla Wraps

2 (9 inch) whole wheat spinach tortillas
Mayonnaise
1 cup shredded cheese
1 (9 ounce) package spring salad mix
1 cup diced, drained tomatoes
4 green onions, finely chopped
1 (4 ounce) package albacore tuna, crumbled

▶ Preheat broiler.

▶ Place tortillas on baking sheet and broil very briefly on each side. Remove from oven and spread mayonnaise on 1 side of tortilla. Sprinkle cheese over tortillas and return to oven just until cheese melts.

▶ Combine salad mix, tomatoes and green onions in bowl and sprinkle on tortillas. Place as much crumbled tuna on tortilla as needed. Roll or fold over to eat. Serves 2.

TIP: Try the Miso Mayo on page 112. It's great.

Homemade Tuna Fish Salad Sandwiches

(See page 144 for Homemade Chicken Salad Meal.)

1 (12 ounce) can tuna fish, drained
½ cup chopped celery
¼ cup green onion, chopped
2 eggs, hard-boiled, finely chopped
Mayonnaise

▶ Drain tuna and put in medium bowl. Add celery, onion, eggs, a little salt and pepper and enough mayonnaise to moisten mixture. Refrigerate and serve. Serves 2.

TIP: If you don't have celery, don't worry about it. If you have some grapes or pecans, throw them in. You don't have to follow any of these salad recipes exactly to have something good. You can replace the tuna with canned wild Alaskan salmon in this for a variation.

Rapid Wrap

4 burrito-size whole wheat tortillas
⅓ cup vinaigrette salad dressing*
4 thin slices deli ham
4 slices Swiss cheese
1½ cups deli coleslaw

▶ Spread tortillas with dressing and add 1 slice ham and 1 slice cheese on each tortilla. Spoon one-fourth coleslaw on top.

▶ Roll and wrap each in wax paper. Place in oven and heat just until cheese begins to melt. Cut wraps in half to serve. Serves 3 to 4.

*TIP: *Homemade vinaigrette is so easy and so much cheaper and better for you than store bought dressings full of low quality polyunsaturated oils and added sugar, corn syrup, high fructose corn syrup and crazy additives. See recipe for Healthy, Fast and Cheap™ Vinaigrette on page 154.*

Sandwich Built for Two

1 (9 inch) round loaf focaccia bread
6 deli ham slices
6 slices Swiss cheese
½ cup chopped, roasted red bell peppers, drained
1 (6 ounce) package baby spinach
⅓ cup romano-basil vinaigrette dressing
2 tablespoons mayonnaise

▶ Preheat oven to 325°.

▶ Place bread on cutting board and slice horizontally. Place layers of ham, cheese, red bell peppers and heavy layer of spinach on bottom half.

▶ Combine vinaigrette dressing and mayonnaise in small bowl and drizzle mixture over spinach layer. Place top of loaf over spinach layer and wrap in foil.

▶ Bake for 15 minutes. Cut focaccia into 4 or 6 wedges and serve immediately. Serves 2 to 3.

Salads

Avocado-Corn Salad

2 ripe avocados, peeled, diced
2 tablespoons fresh lime juice
3 cups grape tomatoes, halved
2 (11 ounce) cans corn, drained
Zesty Italian salad dressing

▶ Place avocados in salad bowl and spoon lime juice and a little salt over avocados. Add tomatoes and corn.

▶ Spoon about ½ cup dressing over salad. Serve 3 to 4.

TIP: Check out canned veggies and make sure you get the ones with no sugar added. If you want to add some color and extra flavor to this recipe, add ½ cup chopped red and green bell peppers.

Broccoli Slaw

1 (16 ounce) package broccoli slaw
1 cup fresh cut broccoli florets
¾ cup Craisins®
1 Granny Smith apple with peel, diced
1 (11 ounce) can mandarin oranges, drained
Poppy seed dressing
½ cup toasted, slivered almonds

▶ Combine broccoli slaw, broccoli florets, Craisins®, apple and oranges in salad bowl. Toss with poppy seed dressing.

▶ Sprinkle almonds on top of salad. Refrigerate for 20 minutes before serving. Serves 4 to 6.

TIP: It's always better to use fresh fruit instead of canned, but it's sure a timesaver.

Broccoli-Noodle Salad

This is a refreshing, crunchy salad that everyone loves.

1 cup slivered almonds, toasted
1 cup sunflower seeds, toasted
2 (3 ounce) package chicken-flavored ramen noodles
1 (12 ounce) package broccoli slaw

▶ Preheat oven to 275°.

▶ Toast almonds and sunflower seeds in oven for 15 minutes.

▶ While toasting, break up noodles in bowl. Serves 6 to 8.

Dressing:

Seasoning packets from ramen noodles
½ cup olive oil
½ cup white vinegar or brown rice vinegar
¼ cup honey

▶ Combine dressing ingredients in small bowl. Pour over noodles,
  almonds, sunflower seeds and broccoli slaw in bowl and mix
  well. Refrigerate for at least 1 hour before serving. (It's even
  better made a day ahead and will stay crisp several days in the
  refrigerator.)

TIP: *Ramen noodles and the seasoning packet are a blank slate
      nutritionally and are not healthy, but they sure are "fast and
      cheap". Better choices are soba noodles found in the Asian section
      of the grocery store. They are whole grain buckwheat. Instead of
      the seasoning packet, use the following ingredients.*

          1 tablespoon toasted sesame oil
          1 tablespoon soy sauce
          1 teaspoon ginger powder
          1 teaspoon garlic powder

Broccoli Salad

5 cups stemmed broccoli florets
1 red bell pepper, seeded, julienned
1 cup chopped celery
1 (8 - 12 ounce) package cubed Monterey Jack cheese
Dressing

▶ Combine all ingredients in bowl and mix well.

▶ Toss with dressing. Refrigerate. Serves 3 to 4.

Red Cabbage Slaw

1 large head red cabbage
2 onions, diced
½ cup coleslaw dressing
½ cup French salad dressing

▶ Slice cabbage very thin and combine with onions in bowl.

▶ In separate bowl, combine dressings, toss with cabbage and onions and refrigerate. Serves 4 to 6.

Carrot Salad

3 cups finely grated carrots
1 (8 ounce) can crushed pineapple, drained or 1 cup fresh
¼ cup flaked coconut
1 tablespoon maple syrup, agave nectar or honey
⅓ cup mayonnaise or sour cream

▶ Combine carrots, pineapple, coconut and sweetener in bowl. Toss with mayonnaise or sour cream and mix well. Refrigerate. Serves 6 to 8.

Cabbage-Carrot Slaw

1 (10 ounce) package coleslaw mix or fresh chopped cabbage
1 (16 ounce) package shredded carrots
2 delicious apples, diced
1 cup Craisins®
⅔ cup chopped walnuts
Poppy seed salad dressing

▶ Combine coleslaw mix, carrots, apples, Craisins® and walnuts in salad bowl. Toss with poppy seed dressing and refrigerate. Serves 4 to 6.

TIP: *Buying whole cabbage is more economical and it is really easy to slice it up for coleslaw. Smash the base of the head on the counter (this loosens the center stem, which is bitter and tough). Cut in half and reserve half for another time. Cut in half again and carefully slice cabbage in long thin strips.*

Carrot and Apple Salad

1 (16 ounce) package shredded carrots
1 green apple with peel, chopped or grated
1 red apple with peel, chopped or grated
½ cup golden raisins
1 tablespoon mayonnaise or sour cream
1 tablespoon lemon juice

▶ Combine carrots, apples and raisins in bowl. Add mayonnaise and lemon juice and toss. Refrigerate. Serves 4.

TIP: *You can grate carrots with a hand grater or food processor with grater attachment. This is definitely "a little time equals a lot of flavor" situation.*

One cup of chopped cabbage has just 22 calories and it is loaded with nutrients, including sulforaphane, a powerful chemical that stops cell-damaging free radicals.

1st Black Bean Quinoa Salad

This is a great high protein vegetarian option.

1 (15 ounce) can black beans
1 (15 ounce) can corn
4 cups cooked quinoa
1 cup finely chopped kale
¼ cup finely chopped cilantro
Healthy, Fast and Cheap™ Vinaigrette (page 154)

▶ Drain beans and corn and toss with quinoa, kale and cilantro. Add dressing to taste and serve. Serves 4.

TIP: *Quinoa is a tiny, bead-shaped grain that contains more protein than any other grain and it has all eight essential amino acids. This is a super grain.*

Colorful English Pea Salad

2 (16 ounce) packages frozen green peas, thawed, drained
1 (12 ounce) package cubed mozzarella cheese
1 red and 1 orange bell pepper, seeded, chopped
1 onion, chopped
1 - 1¼ cups mayonnaise

▶ Combine peas, cheese, bell peppers and onion in large salad bowl; toss to mix.

▶ Stir in mayonnaise, ½ teaspoon each of salt and pepper. Refrigerate. Serves 6 to 8.

Iceberg lettuce has no nutritional value. Choose romaine, butter lettuce, Boston bibb, spinach, kale, chard or any of the leafy greens you see in the produce section.

Green Beans with Tomatoes

2 pounds frozen cut green beans
4 tomatoes, chopped, drained
1 bunch green onions, chopped
1 cup Italian salad dressing

▶ Place beans in saucepan, cover with water and bring to a boil.

▶ Cook for 8 to 10 minutes or until tender-crisp, drain
and refrigerate.

▶ Add tomatoes, green onions and salad dressing and toss to coat.
Serves 6 to 8.

TIP: Check out Healthy, Fast and Cheap™ Vinaigrette on page 154.

Old-Fashioned Potato Salad

6 large potatoes
1 egg, hard-boiled, chopped
1 medium onion, chopped
2 ribs celery, chopped
¼ cup sweet pickle relish, drained
1 large dill pickle, chopped
1½ teaspoons mustard
½ cup mayonnaise

▶ Peel and wash potatoes, cut each potato in 4 to 6 pieces and put
in large saucepan. Cover with water and boil until potatoes are
barely tender.

▶ Cool and cut potatoes into bite-size pieces. Combine cubed
potatoes, egg, onion, celery, pickle relish, dill pickle, mustard,
mayonnaise and a little salt and pepper. Mix well. Refrigerate
and serve. Serves 10 to 12.

Quick Potato Salad

3 - 4 baking potatoes
½ cup pickle relish
3 eggs, hard-boiled, chopped
¾ - 1 cup mayonnaise

▶ Bring 2 quarts of water to a boil while you cut potatoes into small cubes (about the size of common dice) and set in cold water.

▶ Drain potatoes, add to boiling water and cook for 10 minutes (any longer will make them mushy). They may seem underdone, but they will continue to cook after you drain them. Refrigerate.

▶ Add pickle relish, eggs and a little salt and pepper. Stir in mayonnaise. Serves 6 to 8.

TIP: Potatoes can be cooked the night before.

Sour Cream Potato Salad

12 medium new (red) potatoes with peels
1 - 1¼ cups mayonnaise
1 cup sour cream
1 cup chopped fresh green onions with tops

▶ Boil potatoes in medium saucepan until tender for about 20 minutes. Slice potatoes.

▶ Combine mayonnaise, sour cream and 1 teaspoon salt in bowl.

▶ When potatoes are cool, toss with sour cream mixture. Add green onions. Serves 3 to 4.

Cherry Tomato Salad

2 tablespoons red wine vinegar
2 tablespoons olive oil
2 pints cherry tomatoes, halved
1 bunch fresh green onions, chopped
1 small cucumber, peeled, chopped

▶ Combine vinegar, olive oil, 1 teaspoon salt and ½ teaspoon pepper in bowl and mix well.

▶ In separate bowl, combine tomato halves, green onions and cucumber and toss with dressing. Refrigerate. Serves 3 to 4.

Red and Green Salad

3 small zucchini, thinly sliced
2 red delicious apples with peels, chopped
2 cups fresh broccoli florets
¾ cup coarsely chopped walnuts
Creamy Italian salad dressing

▶ Combine zucchini, apples, broccoli and walnuts in salad bowl and toss.

▶ Pour about three-fourths bottle of salad dressing over salad and toss. Use more dressing if needed. Serve immediately. Serves 4 to 6.

TIP: *If you are buying dressing, look for one with olive oil and no added sugar.*

Tossed Zucchini Salad

¾ cup peeled, grated zucchini
1 (6 ounce) package shredded lettuce
½ cup sliced ripe olives
1 carrot, grated
⅓ cup shredded mozzarella cheese
Zesty Italian salad dressing

▶ Toss zucchini, lettuce, olives and carrot in salad bowl. Add cheese and toss with salad dressing. Serves 2 to 4.

TIP: *You can make salad dressing cheaper than you can buy prepared dressings. See pages 153-156 for recipes.*

Boston Bibb Lettuce Salad

1 head Boston bibb lettuce, torn into pieces
1 (11 ounce) can mandarin oranges, drained
⅓ cup walnut pieces

▶ Combine all ingredients in salad bowl. Toss before serving. Serves 3 to 4.

TIP: *If you have time to throw the walnuts in a baking pan, bake them in the oven at 275° for 15 minutes. It really brings out the flavor. It's healthier to use fresh fruits instead of canned fruits and 1 tangerine is great in this recipe.*

Special Spinach Salad

1 (10 ounce) package fresh spinach
1 (16 ounce) can bean sprouts, drained
8 slices Canadian bacon, cooked crisp, chopped
1 (11 ounce) can water chestnuts, chopped
Vinaigrette salad dressing

▶ Combine spinach and bean sprouts in bowl.

▶ When ready to serve, add bacon and water chestnuts and toss
   with vinaigrette salad dressing. Serves 3 to 4.

TIP: *You can make your own vinaigrette salad dressing with 3 parts
olive oil, 2 parts red wine vinegar, and dash of salt and pepper!*

Wilted Spinach-Walnut Salad

2 (8 ounce) packages baby spinach without stems
1 teaspoon minced garlic
2 tablespoons olive oil
½ cup whole walnuts, toasted

▶ Saute spinach and garlic in hot oil in skillet on medium-high heat
   for about 5 minutes or until spinach wilts.

▶ Sprinkle a little salt over spinach and mix. Toss with whole
   toasted walnuts. Serves 4 to 6.

TIP: *If you have time to throw the walnuts in a baking pan, bake them
in the oven at 275° for 15 minutes. It really brings out the flavor.*

Color-Coded Salad

1 (16 ounce) package tri-colored macaroni, cooked, drained
1 red bell pepper, seeded, julienned
1 cup chopped zucchini
1 cup broccoli florets
Caesar salad dressing

▶ Combine all ingredients in bowl. Toss with salad dressing.
   Refrigerate. Serves 3 to 4.

Tri-Color Pasta Salad

3 cups tri-color fusilli (spiral) pasta
1 tablespoon olive oil
1 (8 ounce) package cubed cheddar cheese
1 large bunch broccoli, cut into small florets
1 cup chopped celery
1 cup peeled, cubed cucumber
Ranch salad dressing

▶ Cook pasta according to package directions, drain well and add olive oil to keep pasta from sticking together. Transfer to large salad bowl.

▶ Add cheese, broccoli, celery, cucumber and ample amount of salt and pepper. Toss with salad dressing. Serves 6 to 8.

TIP: *Look for whole grain pastas where you shop. They are much more nutritious.*

Chunky Egg Salad

12 eggs, hard-boiled, quartered
⅓ cup sun-dried tomato mayo
2 ribs celery, sliced
½ cup sliced, stuffed green olives

▶ Place all ingredients in salad bowl and add a little salt and pepper.

▶ Gently toss and serve over bed of lettuce leaves with crackers. Serves 4 to 6.

Also see:

- Homemade Egg Salad Sandwiches on page 117
- Homemade Chicken Salad Meal on page 144
- Homemade Ham or Beef Spread on page 124
- Homemade Tuna Fish Salad Sandwiches on page 126

Homemade Deviled Eggs

6 eggs, hard-boiled
2 tablespoons pickle relish
3 tablespoons mayonnaise
½ teaspoon mustard

▶ Peel eggs and cut in half lengthwise. Remove yolks and mash with fork in bowl. Add relish, mayonnaise, mustard and a little salt and pepper to yolks. Place yolk mixture back into egg white halves. Yields 12 halves.

TIP: If you have some dill pickles and no pickle relish, just cut the pickles in small pieces. It will work.

Elvis's Favorite Peach Salad

1 cup cottage cheese
1 (15 ounce) can peaches halves or slices, drained
Maraschino cherries

▶ Place scoop of cottage cheese in center of each peach half and top with maraschino cherry. Serves 4 to 6.

Crunchy Fruit Salad

2 red apples with peels, chopped
⅓ cup sunflower seeds
½ cup green grapes
⅓ cup plain whole milk yogurt
1 tablespoon maple syrup
1 teaspoon vanilla

▶ Combine apples, sunflower seeds and grapes in bowl.

▶ Add yogurt, maple syrup and vanilla.

▶ Stir to coat salad. Refrigerate before serving. Serves 2.

Late Summer Fresh Fruit Salad

Eat on hot summer days until you are smiling wide!

Sauce:

1 ripe banana
Handful of dates
Handful of almonds
Juice of 1 lemon
Dash of allspice

Salad:

2 cups blueberries
1 cup strawberries
2 apples, cored, sliced thin
2 peaches, pitted, sliced thin
Romaine lettuce

▶ Place banana into blender first. Add rest of sauce ingredients and whip. If this is not enough, add a little water to get blender going.

▶ Mix berries and fruits in bowl and place on romaine leaves. Drizzle sauce over top of fruit salad. Serves 2 to 4.

Nutty Grape-Pineapple Salad

1 pound seedless green grapes, halved
½ cup chopped pecans
⅔ cup shredded cheddar cheese
1 (15 ounce) can pineapple tidbits, drained
½ cup mayonnaise
Lettuce leaves

▶ Combine grapes, pecans, cheese and pineapple in bowl. Fold in mayonnaise. Serve on lettuce leaves. Serves 4 to 6.

Orange-Almond Salad

1 head green leaf lettuce
4 slices Canadian bacon, cooked, diced
1 (11 ounce) can mandarin oranges
⅓ cup slivered almonds, toasted
Vinaigrette dressing

▶ Combine all ingredients in salad bowl. When ready to serve toss with dressing. Serves 3 to 4.

TIP: A healthier choice is fresh fruit such as 2 to 3 tangerines, mandarin oranges, blood oranges or 1 large navel orange.

 # Summer Fruit Salad

1 pound seedless green grapes, halved
3 large peaches, peeled, pitted, sliced thin
4 - 6 plums, peeled, pitted
½ cup chopped pecans
Honey
Lemon juice
Two handfuls of fresh basil leaves, chopped
Lettuce leaves

▶ Combine grapes, peaches, plums and nuts in bowl.

▶ In separate bowl, combine honey, lemon juice and basil leaves. Drizzle over fruit and serve on lettuce leaves. Serves 4 to 6.

www.integrativenutrition.com is a Web site for finding a health counselor in your area and it provides the most amazing nutrition program in the U.S.

Classic Healthy, Fast and Cheap™ Fruit Salad

Buy fruit on sale, preferably organic, preferably local when possible. (Fruit and other produce is on sale at the very peak of harvest. It's a good time to buy the best quality for less.)

1 lime
1 tablespoon honey
Local apples in the fall
Mango (it may not be local, but it is GOOD!)
Banana

For one person, use one of each. Pretty straightforward recipe. I invite you to experiment with sweet spices in this. Cinnamon, cloves, allspice, fennel or even mace, cardamom and ginger.

▶ Squeeze lime and mix with honey in small bowl. Set aside.

▶ Cut apple in half, then half again into quarters. Carefully cut out core.

▶ Slice remaining quarters into four smaller slices and toss in bowl. Cut mango* into chunks and add to bowl.

▶ Slice banana into thick chunks and add to bowl. Lightly toss and drizzle honey-lime mix over fruit. Serves 1.

TIP: *Here's how to cut a mango: Cut off a small section below the bottom of the pit (this is where the mango protrudes slightly), then you can lay the mango down on the flat spot you just cut and slice alongside the flat pit, taking off almost half the mango in one fell swoop. Repeat on the other side and you have most of the meat. Here is the really cool part. Once you have the mango filleted, you simply score the inside of the meat without breaking the skin, like a checker board (vertical and horizontal about 5 times each) then turn the skin inside out inverted and voila! You have mango chunks to simply slice into a bowl.*

Melon Boats

Fresh fruits are perfect for summer entertaining and these little boats make them even more appealing.

2 cantaloupes, chilled
Lettuce leaves
4 cups red and green seedless grapes, chilled
1 cup whole milk yogurt
⅓ cup frozen concentrated orange juice
Lettuce leaves

▶ Cut each melon into 6 lengthwise sections and remove seeds and peel. Place 2 sections on lettuce leaves on separate salad plates.

▶ Heap grapes over and around cantaloupe slices.

▶ Combine yogurt and juice concentrate in bowl and mix well. Ladle over fruit. Serves 6.

Nutty Fruit Salad with Lime Dressing

2 medium apples, cored, sliced into strips
¾ cup halved, seedless green grapes
½ cup chopped celery
¼ cup chopped pecans
½ cup sunflower seeds
2 limes
2 tablespoons honey
½ cup yogurt

▶ Combine apples, grapes, celery, pecans and sunflower seeds in medium bowl.

▶ In separate bowl, squeeze lime juice into honey and add yogurt. Mix well. Drizzle over fruit and serve. Serves 2.

TIP: Limes make any fruit salad sing!

Goji berries or Chinese wolfberry pack a punch of antioxidants, free radicals and essential amino and fatty acids. It is a HIGH energy food.

Congealed Lime-Yogurt Salad

This salad takes a little more time than the following Quick Lime-Yogurt Salad, but it is nutritionally better.

1 package Knorr® gelatin
½ cup frozen apple juice concentrate
Juice of 2 limes
1 (8 ounce) carton plain yogurt
1 (8 ounce) can pear halves (no sugar), drained

▶ Stir gelatin into 1 cup boiling water in bowl. Add apple juice and lime juice and stir until gelatin dissolves.

▶ Divide gelatin mixture into 2 bowls. Blend yogurt into 1 bowl of gelatin and stir pears into other bowl. Set pear mixture aside.

▶ Pour gelatin-yogurt mixture into 9-inch square dish and refrigerate until partially thick.

▶ When gelatin-yogurt mixture thickens partially, pour pears on top. Refrigerate until firm and cut into squares to serve. Serves 4 to 6.

Quick Lime-Yogurt Salad

1 (8 ounce) can pear halves, drained
2 (3 ounce) packages lime gelatin
1 (8 ounce) carton vanilla yogurt

▶ Slice pears.

▶ Stir gelatin into 1½ cups boiling water until it dissolves.

▶ Divide gelatin into 2 bowls. Blend yogurt into 1 bowl of gelatin and stir pears into other bowl. Set pear mixture aside.

▶ Pour gelatin-yogurt mixture into 9-inch square dish and refrigerate until partially thick.

▶ When gelatin-yogurt mixture thickens partially, pour pears on top.

▶ Refrigerate until firm and cut into squares to serve. Serves 4 to 6.

Salad Meals

Homemade Chicken Salad Meal

3 cups cooked, cubed chicken
⅔ cups chopped celery
¾ cup pickle relish
3 eggs, hard-boiled, chopped
¾ cup mayonnaise

▶ Combine chicken, celery, relish and eggs in bowl. Toss with mayonnaise and refrigerate. Serve on lettuce leaves or in sandwiches. Yields 3 to 4 meals.

TIP: *A handful of chopped pecans is a touch of luxury in this salad.*

Chicken Salad Crunch Meal

3 - 4 cups chopped leftover or rotisserie chicken
1 cup chopped celery
1 red bell pepper, seeded, chopped
⅔ cup slivered almonds, toasted
½ cup mayonnaise
1 tablespoon lime juice

▶ Slice chicken breasts into long thin strips. Combine chicken, celery, bell pepper and almonds in bowl.

▶ In separate bowl, combine mayonnaise and lemon juice, stir into salad and toss. Yields 3 to 4 meals.

Fruited Chicken Salad Meal

1 (10 ounce) package spring salad mix
1 cup cooked, chopped chicken
½ cup fresh strawberries
½ cup fresh raspberries
1 fresh peach, sliced
Raspberry salad dressing

▶ Combine salad mix, chicken, strawberries, raspberries and peach in salad bowl. Toss with a little salad dressing. Yields 2 meals.

Quick Chicken Caesar Salad Meal

4 boneless, skinless chicken breast halves, grilled
1 (10 ounce) package romaine salad greens
½ cup shredded parmesan cheese
Caesar salad dressing

▶ Cut chicken breasts into strips. Combine chicken, salad greens, and cheese in large bowl. When ready to serve, toss with salad dressing. Yields 2 to 4 meals.

TIP: *Serve with whole grain bread or one of the toasted breads on pages 101 and 104.*

Cobb Salad Meal

This is a great salad for a meal!

2 boneless, skinless chicken breast halves
6 slices bacon
½ head red leaf lettuce or spring-mix greens
½ head romaine lettuce
1 avocado, peeled, pitted, diced
3 eggs, hard-boiled, diced
2 green onions with tops, chopped
2 tomatoes, diced, drained
¾ cup shredded, sharp cheddar cheese
1 ounce crumbled roquefort or blue cheese
Salad dressing of choice

▶ Boil chicken breast halves in enough water to cover in large saucepan for about 30 minutes or until juices run clear. Cool and dice.

▶ Fry bacon crispy in skillet, drain, cool and crumble.

▶ Tear red leaf and romaine lettuce in small pieces and toss in salad bowl. Arrange each ingredient in its own area on top of lettuce: one area for chicken, one for Canadian bacon, one for avocado, etc.

▶ Sprinkle top with both cheeses or arrange them in their own areas. Refrigerate before serving. Serve with favorite dressing. Yields 2 meals.

Chicken Caesar Salad Meal for Two

The Caesar Salad was created at a restaurant run by Caesar Cardini in Tijuana, Mexico.

The basic idea here is to have cold, dry romaine leaves with chicken, olives, parmesan and dressing on top. This is one of those meals that could be classy very quickly, but if you are in a hurry, it can be very simple.

12 leaves romaine lettuce
2 boneless, skinless chicken breast halves, cooked or grilled
Grated parmesan cheese
½ cup black olives, whole, pitted
Caesar dressing

▶ Chop romaine and place in bowl.

▶ Slice chicken into strips and put it on top.

▶ Sprinkle parmesan and olives on top and serve with dressing. Yields 2 meals.

TIP: *Parmesan cheese is a luxury, but if you spend the $8 for a good hard chunk of parmesan or $5 for the fresh grated carton, you just need a little on top because it is so flavorful. The cheese can be used to garnish many foods (sparingly) and will enhance the experience.*

Quick-Fix-Lunch Meal

3 - 4 boneless, skinless chicken breast halves, cooked, cubed
2 cups fresh broccoli florets
1 red bell pepper, seeded, chopped
1 cup chopped celery
Honey-mustard salad dressing

▶ Combine chicken, broccoli, bell pepper and celery in bowl. Toss mixture with honey-mustard salad dressing and refrigerate. Yields 3 to 4 meals.

TIP: *Serve with whole wheat bread or one of the toasted breads on pages 101 and 104.*

Curried Chicken Salad Meal

Chicken salad is one of those great Healthy, Fast and Cheap™ recipes that incorporates the baked chicken situation. Bake one chicken and you can literally eat all week on the cheap. My personal, all-time favorite chicken salad recipe is also REALLY EASY.

3 cups cooked, cubed chicken
⅔ cup chopped celery
¼ cup sliced black olives
¾ cup mayonnaise
1 tablespoon curry powder
Sprouted or whole grain tortillas
Lettuce, sprouts and tomatoes

▶ Mix it all up and roll it out on some sprouted or whole grain tortillas with lettuce, sprouts or even tomatoes. Yeah, baby! Serves 2 to 4.

Sliced Chicken Combo Meal

1 rotisserie-cooked chicken
¼ cup chopped fresh chives
½ cup chopped pecans
1 cup chopped celery
1 cup chopped green olives, pickles or combination

▶ Skin chicken and cut meat from bones. Slice chicken pieces in thin strips and place in bowl. Add chives, pecans, celery and pickles and mix well. Yields 3 to 4 meals.

Dressing:

2 tablespoons honey
¼ cup extra-virgin olive oil
3 tablespoons white wine vinegar
1 teaspoon chopped fresh thyme

▶ Whisk honey, olive oil, vinegar, thyme, and a little salt and pepper in bowl. Spoon over chicken salad and toss. Refrigerate.

TIP: *You don't have to use the whole chicken for this salad. Reduce the ingredients for just 1 meal and use the remaining chicken for another recipe.*

Stuffed Tomatoes Meal

Homemade Chicken Salad Meal (see page 144)
6 tomatoes
Quick and Crunchy Breadsticks (see page 101)

▶ Make Homemade Chicken Salad Meal recipe on page 144.

▶ Slice enough stem off top of tomatoes to leave large hole. Remove inside of tomatoes, but leave about ¼ to ½-inch on side and bottoms.

▶ Stuff each tomato with about ¾ cup chicken salad.

▶ Make Quick and Crunchy Breadsticks on page 101 and serve with stuffed tomatoes. Serves 6. Yields 4 to 6 meals.

Hawaiian Chicken Daze Meal

3 cups cooked, diced chicken
1 (20 ounce) can pineapple tidbits, well drained
1 cup halved red grapes
3 ribs celery, sliced
1 large ripe banana, sliced

▶ Combine chicken, pineapple, grapes and celery in bowl and toss. Cover and refrigerate. When ready to serve, add banana. Top with dressing and toss. Yields 3 to 4 meals.

Dressing:

½ cup mayonnaise
¾ cup poppy seed dressing
½ cup salted peanuts

▶ Combine mayonnaise, poppy seed dressing and a little salt in bowl.

▶ Just before serving, sprinkle peanuts over top of salad.

Mixed Greens with Chicken and Sun-Dried Tomatoes Meal

2 cups skinned, diced home-baked or rotisserie chicken
1 (10 ounce) package mixed salad greens
½ cup chopped sun-dried tomatoes
1 red bell pepper, seeded, chopped

▶ Combine chicken, greens, tomatoes and bell pepper in salad bowl and toss. Yields 3 to 4 meals.

Dressing:

1 cup vinaigrette salad dressing
2 tablespoons refrigerated honey-mustard salad dressing

▶ Combine vinaigrette dressing and honey-mustard dressing in bowl and pour over salad and toss. (Use more vinaigrette dressing if needed.)

TIP: *You can buy whole chickens cooked on a rotisserie at the deli in most large grocery stores. It's a great timesaver, but baking chicken is about the easiest thing you can do. See Roast Chicken on page 209.*

Mexican Chicken Salad Meal

3 - 4 boneless, skinless chicken breast halves, cooked, cubed
1 (15 ounce) can chick-peas, drained
1 red bell pepper, seeded, diced
1 green bell pepper, seeded, diced
1 cup chopped celery

▶ Combine all ingredients in bowl and serve with dressing below. Yields 3 to 4 meals.

Dressing:

1½ cups sour cream
2 tablespoons chili sauce
2 teaspoons ground cumin
1 small bunch cilantro, minced

▶ Combine all ingredients in bowl and add a little salt and pepper. Pour over chicken salad and toss. Refrigerate before serving.

TIP: *If you've got 3 cups leftover chicken, this is a good place to park it.*

Asian Turkey Salad Meal

1 bunch fresh green onions
¾ pound turkey breast slices
1 (9 ounce) package coleslaw mix
¼ cup chopped fresh cilantro
1 red bell pepper, seeded, julienned

▶ Slice green onion tops in 1-inch pieces; slice white portion thinly. Slice turkey in thin strips. Combine all ingredients in salad bowl. Yields 2 meals.

Dressing:

¼ cup olive oil
2 tablespoons lime juice
1 tablespoon sugar
1 tablespoon peanut butter
1 tablespoon soy sauce

▶ Combine all dressing ingredients in jar with lid. Seal jar and shake dressing until ingredients blend well. Spoon over salad and toss. Serve immediately.

TIP: *When you're in a hurry or you don't have cilantro, go ahead and make the salad. Use the dressing in your refrigerator and no one will know about the cilantro. The important thing is to eat fresh.*

Turkey-Spinach Salad Supper

2 (8 ounce) packages baby spinach without stems
1 cup whole walnuts
½ - 1 cup Craisins®
2 red delicious apples, peeled, sliced
1 pound deli smoked turkey, julienned
½ (15 ounce) bottle refrigerated honey-mustard dressing

▶ Combine spinach, walnuts, Craisins˚, apples and turkey in large salad bowl. Toss salad with half honey-mustard dressing and add more, if needed. Yields 4 meals.

Turkey-Pasta Salad Supper

1 (12 ounce) package tri-color fusilli (spiral) pasta
1 (4 ounce) can sliced ripe olives, drained
1 cup broccoli florets
1 cup cauliflower florets
2 small yellow squash, sliced
1 cup halved cherry tomatoes, drained
1 cup ranch dressing
Hickory-smoked, cracked pepper turkey breast

▶ Cook pasta according to package directions, drain and rinse in cold water. Place in large salad bowl and add olives, broccoli, cauliflower, squash and tomatoes. Toss with dressing.

▶ Cut thin slices of turkey breast and arrange in rows over salad. Serve immediately. Yields 4 meals.

TIP: *You can buy a whole turkey breast, which is about 1 to 1½ pounds. It is more economical in the long run because you will have enough turkey for about 4 to 5 meals. We recommend using whole wheat pasta.*

Taco Salad Meal

1½ pounds ground buffalo or lean ground beef
1 onion, chopped
2 teaspoons chili powder
½ teaspoon ground cumin
1 (14 ounce) can pinto beans or black beans
¾ head romaine lettuce, chopped
3 tomatoes, chopped, drained
1 (16 ounce) package shredded Mexican 4-cheese blend, divided
1 (10 ounce) package blue corn chips
Salsa

▶ Brown meet and onion in skillet; add chili powder and cumin.

▶ Stir beans into meat and cook for additional 5 minutes.

▶ When ready to serve, place lettuce, tomatoes and half cheese in large salad bowl.

▶ Spoon beef-onion mixture over salad, add remaining cheese and chips and toss. Serve with salsa. Yields 3 meals.

Citrus-Tenderloin Salad Meal

1 cup grapefruit sections
1 (10 ounce) package fresh green salad mix
2 cups halved seedless green grapes
1 cup halved fresh strawberries
6 slices leftover cooked pork tenderloin

▶ Drain grapefruit sections and set juice aside. Toss salad mix, green grapes, strawberries and grapefruit sections in salad bowl and arrange salad on individual plates. Slice pork in long strips and place over top. Yields 2 meals.

Dressing:

¼ cup reserved grapefruit juice
2 tablespoons red wine vinegar
2 tablespoons olive oil
2 tablespoons honey
1 tablespoon poppy seeds

▶ Combine all dressing ingredients in jar with lid. Seal jar and shake ingredients until they blend well. Pour dressing over top of individual salads.

Supper Ready Shrimp Salad

2 cups cooked brown rice or any other whole grain
1 (16 ounce) package frozen salad shrimp, thawed
½ cup sliced ripe olives
½ cup chopped celery
1 (8 ounce) bottle zesty Italian salad dressing, divided

▶ Combine brown rice, shrimp, olives and celery in salad bowl. Pour about half salad dressing over salad and toss. Yields 3 meals.

TIP: *Remember to cook a large pot of grains once a week. It is one of the secrets to the Healthy, Fast and Cheap™ lifestyle.*

Making Dressings

Okay, look, if you buy salad dressing, you're spending $100 a year that you don't have to spend. Why not buy something you really want, like new speakers for your iPod? Or better yet, invest the $100.

Now you may be saying, "Yeah, that's great, but I don't know how to make dressing."

No problem, I have got a solution for you.

For between $2.98 and $5.99 (online), you can buy the Healthy Dressings Jar. The glass bottle features six healthy dressing recipes with measurement lines for French Vinaigrette, Italian Herb, Creamy Caesar, Sesame Scallion, Honey Mustard and Creamy Citrus Ginger dressings you make right in the bottle.

Here is the deal. If you make salad dressing at home, you save a lot of money, I mean a LOT of money. But you also dramatically improve the healthy quotient. Now is it faster to grab a bottle of dressing at the store? Yes, but not by much. Once you get the hang of it. You can make homemade dressing in a couple minutes. 1, 2, 3 bang, done!

Salad Dressings

1st Ranch Dressing

Here is the download for simple ranch dressing.

1 part mayo
2 parts plain yogurt
Garlic, dill, chives and salt and black pepper to taste
Dash of Worcestershire sauce

TIP: *Oh, I don't ever really measure these things but I cannot be responsible for the end product. (HINT: If you always eat what you make, you quickly learn to get the ratios right. If you throw out the "mistakes" then it takes lot longer to learn.)*

 # Healthy, Fast and Cheap™ Vinaigrette

*Homemade vinaigrette is so easy and so much cheaper and **better for you** than store bought dressings that are full of low quality polyunsaturated oils and added sugar, corn syrup, high fructose corn syrup and crazy additives.*

3 parts olive oil
1 part apple cider or red wine vinegar
1 part water
2 tablespoons maple syrup or honey
1 teaspoon garlic powder

▶ You can mix this in a jar, bottle, blender or food processor and then store it in an easy-to-pour container (like a recycled cleaned salad dressing bottle!).

TIP: *Variations are made by adding other flavors like 1 teaspoon oregano, basil, sun-dried tomatoes, tomato paste, red peppers, honey dijon-style mustard or raspberry preserves (for raspberry vinaigrette). Experiment with the flavors!*

Homemade Creamy Italian Dressing

▶ Mix up the Healthy Fast and Cheap™ Vinaigrette (page 154) and add in 1 part mayonnaise. It's that easy!

 # Poppy Seed Dressing

1 tablespoon dry mustard
2 - 3 tablespoons finely chopped fresh onion
1 - 2 tablespoons poppy seeds

▶ Really, you can take the Healthy Fat and Cheap™ Vinaigrette recipe (page 154) and turn it into poppy seed dressing by taking out those spices and adding the above ingredients. Simple!

Zesty Italian Dressing

▶ Make up Healthy, Fast & Cheap™ Vinaigrette (page 154).
Add paprika, red pepper and grated parmesan cheese
to taste!

 # Honey-Mustard Dressing

¼ cup honey
¼ cup brown mustard.

▶ Make up the basic Healthy Fast and Cheap™ Vinaigrette
(page 154) and add the above

 # Sun-Dried Tomato Mayo

1 part sun-dried tomatoes
4 parts mayonnaise

▶ Process tomatoes in blender until smooth and fold into
mayonnaise.

*Hydrogenated oils are made from cottonseed, corn
and soybeans, the cheapest oil-producing plants possible.
It is the worst food that we are currently consuming.*

1st Homemade Thousand Island Dressing

This dressing has its roots in an old Russian dressing that aided in digestion. This gets back to those roots. The modern stuff is not going to help with digestion.

1 cup plain yogurt
¼ cup olive oil
1 - 2 tablespoons tomato paste
2 teaspoons lemon juice
2 teaspoons mustard powder
1 tablespoon onion powder
2 teaspoons agave nectar
1 tablespoon chopped pickles or relish

▶ Toss yogurt, olive oil, tomato paste, lemon juice, mustard powder, onion powder, agave nectar, and ½ teaspoon each of salt and pepper in glass bowl. Whisk until they blend well.

▶ Add relish; whisk to combine evenly. Refrigerate for 1 hour. Store in refrigerator for up to 2 weeks in airtight container.

TIP: *Now, for fun, here is the ingredient list of a popular store bought brand of dressing: soybean oil, high fructose corn syrup, water, sour pickle relish (cucumbers, distilled vinegar, salt, turmeric), distilled vinegar, tomato paste, salt, egg yolk, spices, propylene glycol alginate, onion powder, xanthan gum, natural flavors and calcium disodium EDTA.*

Beans and Bean Soups

Here are a few tips to remember when cooking beans. After grains, beans are the next step of the Healthy, Fast and Cheap™ diet. Beans are sometimes a little more difficult for some people to digest. Knowing how to properly prepare beans and legumes can help fight digestive problems. Bringing some variety here will be like a breath of fresh air to your culinary resources. To properly prepare beans, pay attention to the following points.

Rinse beans and remove any stones or extraneous plant matter. Soak beans for at least 6 hours in 4 cups water to 1 cup beans. (Smaller beans need less water and soaking times.) Before cooking, strain off soaking water and rinse beans once more.

Place beans in large pot and add 3 to 4 cups fresh water per 1 cup beans. Bring to a boil then reduce to a simmer. To further improve digestibility, skim off foam after water boils for a few minutes. Kombu seaweed can be added to improve digestion and nutrition. Bay leaf, cumin, garlic and coriander are thought to improve digestibility as well. Always salt your beans near the end of cooking, never at the beginning, so the beans will be soft. Cook beans over low heat until they are soft.

1 Cup Dry Beans	Cooking Time	Cups of Water to 1 Cup Beans
Aduki	1 to 1½ hours	4 to 1
Black-eyed Peas	30 to 45 minutes	4 to 1
Cannellini	1 to 1½ hours	4 to 1
Chick-peas (Garbanzo)	1½ to 2 hours	5 to 1
Great Northern	1 to 1½ hours	4 to 1
Lentils – brown and French	30 to 45 minutes	3 to 1
Lentils - red	20 to 30 minutes	3 to 1
Split Peas	45 minutes	3 to 1
Pinto	1½ - 2 hours	4 to 1
Navy	1½ - 2 hours	4 to 1
Mung	1 hour	3 to 1
Red Kidney	2 to 3 hours	5 to 1

A Basic Pot of Beans

This is a complete meal, especially with a little leftover ham thrown in.

3 cups dried pinto beans
½ pound ham hock or leftover ham
1 onion, chopped
2 tablespoons chili powder
1 tablespoon cumin
1 teaspoon garlic powder

▶ Wash beans, cover with water in large pot and soak overnight.

▶ Drain beans and cover again with water. Add another 3 inches of water to pot. Add all ingredients.

▶ Bring to a boil. Reduce heat and cook on medium-low in covered pot for about 3 hours or until beans are tender. Be sure to check pot and add water if needed. Add salt and pepper if needed. Serves 10 to 14.

TIP: *Leftover beans are great for bean dip and refried beans. Drain and mash them. Check out Black Been Salso on page 51 or Frijoles Refritos on page 52 for seasonings.*

HINT: *To make beans easy to digest, remember to use one of the following traditional foods or spices: garlic, cumin, ginger, kombu (sea vegetable) or fennel.*

Lucky Pea Soup

1 onion, chopped
Olive oil or butter
1 cup cooked, cubed ham
1 (15 ounce) can black-eyed peas with jalapenos with liquid
1 (14 ounce) can chicken broth
1 teaspoon minced garlic
1 teaspoon dried sage

▶ Saute onion with a little oil in large saucepan. Add ham, black-eyed peas, broth, garlic and sage and cook on high heat.

▶ Bring to a boil, reduce heat and simmer for 20 minutes. Stir occasionally. Serves 4 to 6.

1ˢᵗ My Favorite Healthy Fast and Cheap™ Soup

Again, there is no wrong way to make this soup, but I have supplied a basic recipe to help you get started.

1 (16 ounce) package frozen mixed vegetables
2 bouillon cubes
1 (15 ounce) can white beans

▶ This is so easy that it's ridiculous. You come home, open a bag of vegetables and drop them into a pot. Add 3 cups water and bouillon cubes. Heat on medium for 15 minutes and you're done. Serves 2.

Here are a couple of additional pointers to get you to delicious right off the bat.

- Use a variety blend of vegetables. Every grocery store has them: Asian blend, Italian blend or garden blend. For example, you can get a mix of mushrooms, baby corn, broccoli and green beans.

- Use a natural bouillon. My choice is Rapunzel because it is very tasty. Avoid commercial bouillon that is rich in monosodium glutamate.

- Add beans for heartiness.

- If you want, you can include lean ground beef or ground buffalo (browned in skillet) for a fuller soup. It is so easy. Just include it at the same time as everything else, but take a minute to break up the clumps into small pieces.

- Noodles are another way to make this more substantial. (Soba noodles always come packaged in equal-sized bunches. I call these a round or bolt.)

- I make this a complete meal by adding browned ground buffalo and a round of soba noodles. Yum! Serves 4.

Navy Bean Soup

3 (16 ounce) cans navy beans with liquid
1 (14 ounce) can chicken broth
1 cup cooked, chopped ham
1 large onion, chopped
½ teaspoon garlic powder
Cornbread (pages 103-104)

▶ Combine all ingredients in large saucepan, add 1 cup water and
  bring to a boil.

▶ Simmer until onion is tender-crisp and serve hot with cornbread.
  Serves 6 to 8.

TIP: *Some of the cornbread recipes in this cookbook are very hearty
and could easily make a meal by themselves.*

Chicken Soups

Creamy Chicken-Spinach Soup

1 (9 ounce) package refrigerated cheese tortellini
2 (14 ounce) cans chicken broth, divided
1 (10 ounce) can cream of chicken soup
1 (12 ounce) can white chicken meat with liquid
1 (10 ounce) package frozen chopped spinach
2 cups milk
½ teaspoon dried thyme

▶ Cook tortellini in soup pot with 1 can chicken broth according to
  package directions.

▶ Stir in remaining can broth, soup, chicken, spinach, milk,
  1 teaspoon salt, ½ teaspoon pepper and thyme. Bring to boil,
  reduce heat to low and simmer for 10 minutes. Serves 4 to 6.

Basic Homemade Chicken Soup

Roast Chicken (see page 209)
3 carrots, chopped
1 onion, chopped
2 potatoes, chopped
3 ribs celery, chopped
6 cloves garlic, minced

▶ Prepare Roast Chicken recipe on page 209.

▶ When cool, separate meat from bones and refrigerate meat. Put bones in slow cooker or heavy soup pot and cover with water.

▶ Simmer for 8 to 24 hours on lowest setting. Check to make sure bones are always covered with water. Cool and strain.

▶ Add veggies and garlic to stock and bring to a boil. Simmer for 20 minutes.

▶ Chop meat and add to soup. Cook for additional 10 minutes.

▶ Serve with salt and pepper to taste. Serves 6 to 8.

TIP: Now you have a big old pot of chicken soup to eat for the week. With practice, this can become really easy for you.

 # Real Quick Chicken Noodle Soup

3 (14 ounce) cans chicken broth
1 (15 ounce) can sliced carrots, drained
1 cup sliced celery
⅔ cup medium egg noodles
2 cups cooked, diced chicken or turkey

▶ Combine all ingredients in large saucepan and bring to a boil.

▶ Reduce heat and simmer for 15 minutes or until noodles are done. Serves 4 to 6.

1st Creamy Cauliflower, Chicken and Rice Soup

1 (10 ounce) package frozen cauliflower
1 (14 ounce) can chicken broth
1 (14 ounce) can coconut milk (not low-fat)
1 cup cooked brown rice
1½ cups cooked, chopped chicken or turkey

▶ Combine cauliflower and broth in saucepan, bring to a boil and simmer for 10 minutes. Remove from heat.

▶ Add coconut milk to blender, carefully add cauliflower-broth mixture and blend until creamy.

▶ Add brown rice and pulse a few times (just enough to break up grain a little). Add more water if necessary.

▶ Return to cooking pot, add chicken and simmer until hot. Serves 4.

TIP: *The healthiest chicken broth is to make your own chicken stock as in Basic Homemade Chicken Soup on page 161. The second healthiest way is mix 2 cups water with 2 Rapunzel bouillon cubes.*

Hearty 15-Minute Turkey Soup

1 (14 ounce) can chicken broth
3 (15 ounce) cans navy beans with liquid
1 (28 ounce) can stewed tomatoes with liquid
3 cups cooked, cubed white turkey meat
2 teaspoons minced garlic
1 (6 ounce) package baby spinach, stems removed
Freshly grated parmesan cheese

▶ Combine broth, beans, stewed tomatoes, turkey, garlic and a little salt and pepper in soup pot. Bring to a boil, reduce heat and simmer on medium heat for about 10 minutes.

▶ Stir in baby spinach, bring to a boil and cook, stirring constantly, for 5 minutes. When ready to serve, sprinkle each serving with grated parmesan cheese. Serves 6 to 8.

Quick Asian-Style Chicken-Noodle Soup

2 cups chicken broth
2 tablespoons sesame oil
1 round soba noodles, broken
2 cubes bouillon
1 (10 ounce) package frozen Asian-style vegetables
½ cup sliced fresh or canned mushrooms
3 cups cooked, cubed chicken or turkey

▶ Boil 2 cups water in large saucepan. Add broth, oil, soba noodles, bouillon and Asian-style frozen vegetables.

▶ Heat to boiling, reduce heat to medium and cook for about 5 minutes. Stir in mushrooms and chicken and continue cooking over medium heat until all ingredients are thoroughly hot. Serves 4 to 6.

High quality fats include olive oil, coconut oil, organic butter, high quality cold-pressed sesame oil, almond oil, macadamia nut oil or other cold-pressed oils.

Veggie Soups

 ## The Ultimate Healthy, Fast and Cheap™ Lunch for People on the Go!

I can't take credit for this idea. Two Naropa students suggested it in the newspaper. Here are the basics.

1 Thai Kitchen® rice noodle soup packet
Broccoli crown, chopped into small pieces
1- 2 eggs

▶ Bring the correct volume of water to a boil and add noodles, seasoning from package and broccoli pieces.

▶ After 1 minute crack and drop in 1 or 2 eggs. Boil for 1 additional minute with gentle stirring and voila, Healthy, Fast and Cheap™ in 5 minutes. Serves 1.

TIP: *Thai Kitchen® noodles come in many varieties and you can add any green vegetable you like. Kale, collard greens and broccoli are among my favorites, but celery, green onions, cilantro or any other vegetable can be used. Get innovative. The egg can stay or go, but remember that this adds to the nutritional value of the meal. Sliced tofu can also be added for a veggie version or you may elect to add leftover chicken.*

 # Potato-Leek Soup

2 (14 ounce) cans chicken broth seasoned with garlic
2 potatoes, peeled, cubed
1 cup finely chopped leeks
6 pieces Canadian bacon, cooked, crumbled

▶ Combine broth, potatoes and leeks in large saucepan. Bring to a boil, reduce heat to medium-high and boil for about 15 minutes or until potatoes are tender.

▶ Season with a little pepper. Ladle into bowls and sprinkle with crumbled Canadian bacon. Serves 4.

TIP: *Leeks are like big green onions, ask your produce person at your supermarket about them.*

Potato-Sausage Soup

1 pound pork sausage links
1 cup chopped celery
1 cup chopped onion
2 (10 ounce) cans potato soup
1 (14 ounce) can chicken broth

▶ Cut pork sausage in 1-inch diagonal slices. Brown in large, heavy skillet, drain and remove to separate bowl. Leave sausage drippings in skillet and saute celery and onion. Drain. Return celery and onion to skillet.

▶ Add 1 cup water, potato soup, chicken broth and cooked sausage slices. Bring to a boil and simmer on low for 20 minutes. Serves 4.

TIP: The healthiest version of this would replace the potato soup with 2 cups diced potatoes and ½ cup whipping cream.

Fiesta Vegetable Soup

1 (15 ounce) can Mexican stewed tomatoes
1 (15 ounce) can whole kernel corn
1 (15 ounce) can pinto beans
2 (14 ounce) cans chicken broth
1 (10 ounce) bag frozen mixed vegetables
½ - 1 cup shredded cheddar cheese

▶ Combine tomatoes, corn, pinto beans, chicken broth, vegetables and a little salt in soup pot on high heat and mix well.

▶ Stir in cheese and cook until veggies are tender-crisp. Serves 4 to 6.

TIP: The healthier version of this replaces cheddar cheese with queso fresco or queso blanco. Queso fresco (literally, fresh cheese) is crumbly and queso blanco melts better, more like Monterey Jack.

1st Quick Cream of Broccoli Soup

1 (10 ounce) package frozen broccoli
2 bouillon cubes
1 (14 ounce) can coconut milk
Grated parmesan cheese

▶ Boil 1 cup water in saucepan, add broccoli and cook on medium heat for 5 minutes.

▶ Add bouillon and stir until it dissolves. Turn off heat.

▶ Pour coconut milk in blender.

▶ Carefully add broccoli and cooking liquid to blender. Slowly and carefully process until creamy. Sprinkle with parmesan cheese. Serves 2.

Warm-Your-Soul Soup

Great flavor — great soup!

3 (15 ounce) cans chicken broth
1 (10 ounce) can Italian stewed tomatoes with liquid
½ cup chopped onion
¾ cup chopped celery
½ (12 ounce) box fettuccini

▶ Combine chicken broth, tomatoes, onion and celery in large soup pot, bring to a boil and simmer until onion and celery are almost done.

▶ Add fettuccini and cook according to package directions. Season with a little salt and pepper. Serves 4 to 6.

Spicy Tomato Soup

2 (10 ounce) cans tomato soup
1 (15 ounce) can Mexican stewed tomatoes
Sour cream

▶ Combine soup and stewed tomatoes in saucepan and heat. To serve, place dollop of sour cream on top of soup. Serves 4.

Hearty Soups

Beef-Noodle Soup

1 pound lean ground beef
1 (46 ounce) can tomato juice
1 (16 ounce) package frozen mixed vegetables
2 tablespoons soy sauce
1 tablespoon onion powder
1 package onion-flavored Thai Kitchen® rice noodles

▶ Cook beef in large saucepan over medium heat until no longer pink and drain.

▶ Stir in tomato juice, mixed vegetables, soy sauce and onion powder and bring to a boil.

▶ Reduce heat and simmer for 6 minutes or until vegetables are tender. Return to boil and stir in noodles. Cook for 3 minutes or until noodles are tender and serve hot. Serves 4.

Easy Meaty Minestrone

3 cups tomato juice
1 (15 ounce) can garbanzo beans
1 (10 ounce) package frozen mixed vegetables
1 (15 ounce) can pinto beans with juice
1 pound ground buffalo or beef
1 (5 ounce) package grated parmesan cheese

▶ Combine tomato juice, garbanzo beans, vegetables, pinto beans and beef with ½ cup water in large saucepan.

▶ Bring to a boil, reduce heat to low and cook for about 15 minutes. To serve, sprinkle each serving with parmesan cheese. Serves 6 to 8.

Spaghetti Soup

1 (7 ounce) package whole grain spaghetti
1 (18 ounce) package frozen, cooked meatballs, thawed
1 (28 ounce) jar spaghetti sauce
1 (15 ounce) can Mexican stewed tomatoes

▶ Cook spaghetti with 3 quarts boiling water and a little salt in soup pot for about 6 minutes (no need to drain).

▶ When spaghetti is done, add meatballs, spaghetti sauce and stewed tomatoes and cook until mixture is thoroughly hot. Serves 4 to 5.

TIP: See No-Fuss Meatballs on page 64 for a healthier way to have meatballs.

Quick Enchilada Soup

1 pound lean ground beef, browned, drained
1 (15 ounce) can Mexican stewed tomatoes
2 (15 ounce) cans pinto beans with liquid
1 onion, chopped
2 (10 ounce) cans enchilada sauce
1 (8 ounce) package shredded 4-cheese blend

▶ Combine beef, tomatoes, beans, onion, enchilada sauce and 1 cup water in soup pot.

▶ Bring to a boil, reduce heat and simmer for 35 minutes. When serving, sprinkle a little shredded cheese over each serving. Serves 4.

Super Quickie Gumbo

½ (10 ounce) bag frozen chopped onions and bell peppers
½ (10 ounce) bag frozen okra
1 cup tomato sauce
1 (14 ounce) can chicken broth
½ pound turkey sausage, broken up
1 (6 ounce) can white crabmeat, flaked
1 (6 ounce) can tiny shrimp, drained
File gumbo, garlic, thyme, pepper and sea salt
Brown rice or quinoa

► Combine all ingredients with 2 cups water in saucepan. Cover and simmer for 15 minutes. Season according to taste.

► Serve over brown rice or quinoa. Serves 2 to 4.

TIP: *Any recipe can be tweaked, adjusted and made to match what you have on hand. Don't ever feel like you need to have all the ingredients. Just make substitutions or subtractions and you'll learn what you like even faster!*

Chili-Soup Warmup

1 (1 pound) lean ground beef
1 (10 ounce) can Italian tomato sauce
1 (10 ounce) can chili beans or pinto beans, drained
1(15 ounce) can chicken broth

► Brown meat in skillet until it is no longer pink and drain well. Transfer to large saucepan and add tomato sauce, chili beans and broth.

► Cook over medium heat and add water for desired thickness of soup. Cook for about 15 minutes. Serves 4.

Easy Chili

4 pounds lean ground beef
2 (10 ounce) packages hot chili mix
1 (6 ounce) can tomato sauce
2 (15 ounce) cans stewed tomatoes with liquid
2½ teaspoons ground cumin

▶ Break ground beef into pieces, brown in large skillet and drain. Transfer beef to 5 to 6-quart slow cooker.

▶ Add chili mix, tomato sauce, stewed tomatoes, cumin, 1 teaspoon salt and 1 cup water.

▶ Cover and cook on LOW for 4 to 5 hours. Serves 6 to 8.

TIP: You can make your own chili seasoning if you have time.

¼ cup flour
½ - 1 cup chili powder
3 tablespoons salt
½ cup onion powder
¼ cup garlic powder
2 tablespoons cumin
2 tablespoons oregano

Championship Chili

2 pounds beef chuck roast, cubed or lean ground meat
2 tablespoons olive oil
1 onion, chopped
3 cloves garlic, chopped
1 (8 ounce) can tomato sauce
1 cup beef broth
5 tablespoons chili powder
2 teaspoons ground cumin

▶ Brown beef in hot oil in large, heavy saucepan. Stir in onion, garlic, tomato sauce and beef broth. Stir to mix well.

▶ Add chili powder, cumin, and ½ teaspoon each of salt and pepper and stir well.

▶ Cover and simmer for 1 to 2 hours and stir occasionally. If liquid is too thin, remove cover and continue simmering. Serves 4 to 6.

TIP: Add 1 (15 ounce) can pinto beans if you like beans in chili.

Meat and Potato Stew

2 pounds beef stew meat
Butter
4 cups diced potatoes
2 cups diced carrots
2 bouillon cubes

▶ Sprinkle salt and pepper over stew meat. Cook in skillet with butter to brown outside. (Inside will be red.) Drain and transfer to large saucepan. Add 2 cups water and cook for 1 hour over medium heat. Add water if necessary.

▶ Add potatoes, carrots and bouillon and mix well. Heat to a boil, reduce heat and cook on low for 30 minutes. Season with salt and pepper. Serves 4 to 6.

Quick Brunswick Stew

1 (15 ounce) can beef stew
1 (15 ounce) can chicken stew
1 (15 ounce) can lima beans with liquid
2 (15 ounce) cans stewed tomatoes with liquid
1 (15 ounce) can whole kernel corn
½ teaspoon hot sauce, divided

▶ Combine beef stew, chicken stew, beans, tomatoes and corn in large stew pot. Bring stew to boiling on medium-high heat, reduce heat and cook on low for 20 minutes.

▶ Brunswick stew needs to be a little spicy, so stir in ¼ teaspoon hot sauce and taste. Add more if needed. If you don't want spicy, add 1 tablespoon Worcestershire sauce to stew. Serves 6.

TIP: *For the healthiest choice, look for soups with no added preservatives, flavor enhancers like monosodium glutamate, and hydrolyzed corn protein or added sugar.*

Pizzas

Deep-Dish Pizza

2 (13 ounce) packages refrigerated pizza dough
1 cup chopped red onion
2 tablespoons olive oil
1 (10 ounce) package frozen chopped spinach, thawed, drained*
1 cup ricotta cheese
1 cup shredded mozzarella cheese, divided
3 roma tomatoes, sliced

▶ Preheat oven to 400°.

▶ Unroll 1 package pizza dough and gently pull into 12-inch circle. Place dough on sprayed baking sheet and bake for 5 minutes.

▶ Cook onion in oil in saucepan and add spinach with a little salt and pepper. Cook for 2 minutes and spread over partially baked crust.

▶ Combine ricotta cheese and ¼ cup mozzarella cheese in small bowl.

▶ Spread ricotta mixture over spinach layer and top with tomato slices. Sprinkle remaining cheese over top.

▶ Unroll remaining pizza dough and place on top. Pinch together edges of dough and bake for 20 minutes or until top is golden. Cut in wedges to serve. Serves 3 to 4.

*TIP: *Squeeze spinach between paper towels to completely remove excess moisture.*

Gourmet Pizza

2 large sweet onions, thinly sliced*
1 (12 ounce) refrigerated pizza crust
10 medium sun-dried tomatoes without oil
3 ounces gorgonzola cheese
10 - 20 spinach leaves, washed, dried

▶ Preheat oven to 425°.

▶ Spray large non-stick pan and warm over medium heat. Add onions and reduce heat to medium-low. Cook for 15 to 20 minutes, stirring frequently, until onions brown.

▶ Prepare pizza crust according to package directions. Mince tomatoes, crumble cheese and tear spinach into pieces in bowl; set aside.

▶ Spread caramelized onions on pizza crust and bake for 12 minutes.

▶ Remove from oven and add tomatoes, spinach and cheese. Bake for additional 3 minutes or until cheese melts. Serve with freshly ground pepper. Serves 4.

*TIP: Look for Texas SuperSweet 1015 onions or Vidalia® onions from Georgia. They are very sweet and taste great.

Caesar Salad Pizza

1 (12 inch) prepared Italian pizza crust
2¾ cups shredded mozzarella cheese, divided
1 cup cooked, chopped chicken
2 cups shredded romaine lettuce
½ (8 ounce) bottle Caesar dressing

▶ Preheat oven to 400°.

▶ Top pizza crust with 2 cups mozzarella cheese and bake for 8 minutes or until cheese melts.

▶ Combine chicken, lettuce and remaining cheese with dressing in bowl and toss. Top hot pizza with salad and cut into wedges. Serves 2.

TIP: This is a great recipe for leftover chicken.

Southwest Pizza

1 (12 inch) package flour tortillas
¾ cup Easy Gringo Guacamole (see page 51)
1¼ cups cooked, chopped chicken
½ cup roasted red peppers, drained, sliced
1 (4 ounce) can sliced ripe olives, drained
1 (8 ounce) package shredded Mexican 4-cheese blend

▶ Preheat oven to 350°.

▶ Place tortillas on oiled baking sheet and spread Easy Gringo Guacamole over each. Top with chicken, red peppers and olives and spread evenly. Top with cheese.

▶ Bake for 15 minutes or just until cheese bubbles and is light brown. Cut pizza into wedges to serve. Serves 1.

TIP: *For the healthiest way to eat pizza, use whole wheat or sprouted grain tortillas for the crust.*

Sausage Pizza

½ pound turkey or pork sausage
1 (12 ounce) can Italian-style tomato paste
1 (10 ounce) package frozen spinach, thawed, drained well*
1 (10 ounce) package refrigerated pizza dough
½ cup shredded mozzarella cheese

▶ Preheat oven to 400°.

▶ Brown sausage in skillet and stir to break up pieces. Drain fat, add tomato paste and drained spinach and heat until bubbly.

▶ Unroll pizza dough, place on flat surface and pat into 8 x 12-inch rectangle. Cut into 6 squares.

▶ Divide sausage mixture evenly among squares and sprinkle with cheese. Lift one corner of each square and fold over filling to make triangle.

▶ Press edges together with tines of fork to seal. Bake for about 12 minutes or until light golden brown. Serve immediately. Serves 2.

*TIP: *Squeeze spinach between paper towels to completely remove excess moisture.*

Chicken Pizza

4 (8 inch) flour or whole wheat tortillas
2 cups cooked, diced chicken breast
1 (11 ounce) can Mexicorn®, drained
1 (15 ounce) can black beans, rinsed, drained
Olive oil
2 tablespoons lemon or lime juice
1½ cups Monterey Jack cheese with jalapeno peppers

▶ Preheat oven to 350°. Place tortillas on sprayed baking sheet and bake for 10 minutes or until edges are light brown. Remove from oven, stack and press down to flatten.

▶ Combine chicken, corn and black beans with a little oil in skillet. Heat, stirring constantly, until mixture is thoroughly hot. Stir in lemon juice.

▶ Place tortillas on baking sheet and spoon about ¾ cup chicken-corn mixture on each tortilla. Sprinkle cheese on top of each pizza and return to oven for 2 minutes or just until cheese melts. Serves 2 to 4.

TIP: *We use leftover chicken or buy about 1 pound thinly sliced smoked chicken breast at the deli and chop some of it up for this dish. You don't have to have 2 cups. Use whatever you've got.*

Barbecued Pizza

1 (12 inch) prepared pizza crust
1 (12 ounce) package Mexican shredded cheese, divided
½ - 1 pound shredded barbecued beef
1 (4 ounce) sliced ripe olives, drained

▶ Preheat oven to 400°.

▶ Place pizza crust on baking sheet and sprinkle half cheese over crust. Spread shredded barbecued beef over top of cheese and sprinkle remaining cheese over top. Arrange olives over top of pizza.

▶ Bake for 5 to 10 minutes or until hot and bubbly. Serves 2.

TIP: *Another healthy choice for pizza crust is 4 slices whole wheat or sprouted grain bread.*

Planet Pizza

1 (8 ounce) package crescent dinner rolls
1 (8 ounce) can tomato sauce
½ pound sliced Canadian bacon, diced
½ cup sliced fresh mushrooms
1 teaspoon ground oregano
1 cup shredded mozzarella cheese

▶ Preheat oven to 375°.

▶ Spread crescent dinner roll dough on baking sheet; seal seams and perforations. Spread tomato sauce over dough evenly and sprinkle Canadian bacon over tomato sauce.

▶ Sprinkle with mushrooms, oregano and cheese. Bake for 5 to 10 minutes or until cheese bubbles. Serves 1 to 2.

1st Tortilla Pizza

1 (12 ounce) can Italian-style tomato paste
4 whole wheat tortillas
1 (3.5 ounce) package pepperoni slices
1 (8 ounce) package shredded mozzarella cheese

▶ Preheat oven to 375°.

▶ Mix tomato paste with enough water to make desired consistency. Lay tortillas on baking sheet. Spread tomato paste over each tortilla.

▶ Arrange 8 pepperoni slices on each tortilla. Top with cheese. Place on sprayed baking sheet and bake for 5 to 10 minutes or until cheese melts. Serves 2.

TIP: *Make your sauce from tomato paste. It is SO MUCH cheaper than buying prepared sauces. I like to use the paste without diluting it so it is really rich and tomatoey.*

Keep Going

Rice and Grains
Pasta
Veggies

Leaving Home Cookbook
and Survival Guide

Keep Going Contents

Dinner

In our culture, dinner is the central meal of the day. In this section I will offer some useful tips and ideas for this meal. The foundation of these meals will be whole grains.

Rice and Grains

The significant difference between morning cereal and an evening grain is the amount of water used for each. The general rules for grains are as follow.

Grain	Time	Amount of Grain to Water
Long-Grain Brown Rice	45 minutes	1 to 2
Short-Grain Brown Rice	40 minutes	1 to 2
Whole-Grain Basmati Rice	40 minutes	1 to 2
Whole-Grain Jasmine Rice	40 minutes	1 to 2
Basmati Rice	20 minutes	1 to 2
Jasmine Rice	20 minutes	1 to 2
Medium-Grain Brown	40 minutes	1 to 2
Medium-Grain White	15 minutes	1 to 2
Long-Grain White Rice	20 minutes	1 to 2
Short-Grain White Rice	15 minutes	1 to 2
Quinoa	15 minutes	1 to 2
Millet	30 minutes	1 to 2.5
Amaranth	20 minutes	1 to 2
Buckwheat	15 minutes	1 to 2
Pearled Barley	60 minutes	1 to 2
Whole Grain Rye	60 minutes	1 to 2
Whole Grain Wheat	60 minutes	1 to 2
Whole Grain Kamut	60 minutes	1 to 2
Whole Grain Oats	60 minutes	1 to 2
Polenta (Corn Grits)	10 to 20 minutes	1 to 3

Cooking times and ratio of water to grain are contingent on soaking the grain 6 to 8 hours before cooking.

I have friends who tell me, "Cooking grains takes too long." While it is true that brown rice takes 40 to 50 minutes to cook, it takes only minutes of your time to prepare it!

You take it one step at a time.

Put some rice in a bowl and add enough water to completely cover it. (If you can, put a bit of yogurt or whey in there.) Later (4 to 24 hours), drain the grain in a fine wire strainer.

Place the grain in a pot and cover with water to about ½ inch above the surface. Bring to a boil, then immediately reduce to a simmer for the appropriate amount of time.

Your total involvement amounts to under 10 minutes and is probably closer to 5 minutes. It's as simple as soak, drain, cover, boil, simmer and you're done.

You'll need a timer to pull this off and for $5 you can get a kitchen timer that will "ding" when the grain is cooked. This is a great investment that will help you with all your cooking.

By the way, you have my permission to burn the rice. Yeah, go ahead and have some catastrophes in the kitchen. By making mistakes, you learn.

Here are a few tips to remember with rice and beans.

- It is essential to soak the beans.

- Preparation time is minimal, but most beans need to cook for a couple of hours. Lentils, mung beans and other small beans don't need as much cooking time.

- Use traditional recipes and try thousands of variations.

- Add a little meat or fish to bean dishes to maximize the protein delivery. (This is standard practice in most traditional bean-eating cultures. A little animal protein completes the protein in beans in a beautiful way.)

- You can really get by with a lot of fried rice when you're out on your own. It is the flagship Healthy, Fast and Cheap™ way to go. I mean, hey, how much does rice cost? And, fried rice taste great! The hard-core health nut might argue that it is fried and fried foods should be avoided, but it is better than drive-through and you want to eat healthy food that TASTES GOOD!

- Why soak grains? Soaking grains removes the phytic acid that prevents absorption of minerals and makes grains more difficult to digest.

- Does the digit thing really work? Yes. I learned this from the owner of an Asian food store in Ft. Myers, Florida, and it has been confirmed many times by grain experts. You just put your grain in a saucepan, pour on water, shake the grain down so it is even all around, and then add enough water so that it covers the grain up the first joint of your index finder. Simple. I never measure water for cooking grains and it always turns out great.

(1st) Beans and Rice

This Healthy, Fast and Cheap™ recipe can be your salvation.

3 cups black beans
1 piece kombu (Japanese seaweed)
1 (6 ounce) can tomato paste
2 teaspoons cumin

▶ Before you go to bed, place 3 cups black beans in bowl with 9 cups water (3 times the amount of beans). Let soak overnight and into the next day. The beans will need from 30 minutes to 20 hours to soak, depending on the bean.

▶ The next afternoon, drain beans and place in pot. Cover with water. Add in kombu. (This will promote digestion of the beans and serve as an excellent source of trace minerals.) Turn the heat on low and let it go.

▶ In 1 hour check the tenderness of beans. Add tomato paste, cumin, dash of pepper and a little salt. (Remember, don't salt the beans until they are close to done or they'll get tough!) Serve with Fried Rice (see page 184), avocado and fresh cilantro. Serves 2.

1st Rice and Dal

Dal [dahl} is a Hindi word for legumes such as lentils, peas and beans. It is also used for thick soups and stews made with legumes.

2 cups lentils
2 cups rice
Butter
Curry powder
Carrots, chopped

▶ Soak lentils in water for 2 hours, drain and rinse. Cook over medium heat until beans get tender and hot. Prepare rice according to package directions. Cook lentils with butter, curry powder and carrots. Salt to taste near end of cooking. Serves 2.

 # 1st Cannellini Beans

1 (14 ounce) can cannellini beans
1 Italian sausage
2 roma tomatoes
1 sweet onion, chopped
Rice, cooked

▶ Cook cannellini beans over medium heat until they get tender and hot. Once beans begin to get tender, chop Italian sausage, roma tomatoes and some onion and throw them into the pot. Cook for about 20 minutes. Serve over rice. Serves 2.

The center of your diet should be whole grains, beans, legumes, eggs and leafy green veggies.

Arroz con Gandules

This Puerto Rican classic is jammin'.

Dry pigeon peas
1 onion, chopped
1 bell pepper, seeded, chopped
1 teaspoon minced garlic
1 (8 ounce) can tomato sauce
Rice, cooked

▶ Prepare pigeon peas according to package directions or buy a ready-to-go can. (See Rice and Dal on page 182 for instructions.)

▶ Once beans are tender, toss into pot with onion, bell pepper, garlic, tomato sauce and a little pepper. Simmer for additional 30 minutes. Serve over rice. Serves 2.

Brown Rice and Chicken Casserole

Brown rice has so many variations. Here are some of the Healthy, Fast and Cheap™ ways you can get it on with the main grain. These are great ways to use leftover brown rice.

2 cups cooked brown rice
½ cup chopped onion
½ cup chopped mushrooms
2 generous tablespoons olive oil
¼ cup coconut milk
2 medium boneless, skinless chicken breast halves

▶ Preheat oven to 300°.

▶ Throw rice, onion, mushrooms, olive oil, coconut milk and a little pepper in bowl. Stir well. Add milk if necessary to make consistency a little wet.

▶ Lay chicken in baking dish and cover with rice mixture. Bake for 2 hours 30 minutes. Serves 1.

TIP; If you want to make this to share with your housemates, increase the amount of everything in the recipe and bake in a bigger dish.

Easy Brown Rice

1 cup brown rice
1 (10 ounce) can French onion soup
1 (15 ounce) can beef broth
3 tablespoons butter, melted

▶ Preheat oven to 350°.

▶ Put rice in baking dish. Pour soup, broth and butter on top.

▶ Cover and bake for 50 minutes. Serves 1 to 2.

 # Fried Rice

This is the standby for many cultures around the planet. Here I provide a basic method and it couldn't be simpler!

2 tablespoons butter or coconut oil
Onion, diced
Bell pepper, seeded, diced
Celery, diced
2 cups cooked brown rice

▶ Heat butter or oil in pan on medium heat. Add vegetables and saute. Add a little salt and pepper. As veggies begin to brown, stir in cooked rice. Saute with rice for 5 to 10 minutes. Serves 2 to 3.

TIP: *You can go South American with this by adding in chili, cumin, cilantro, tomato paste or adobo. You get a Thai flavor going with some fish sauce, ginger, cilantro or basil. Experiment on your own.*

Pecan-Rice Pilaf

½ cup pecan pieces
3 tablespoons butter, melted
1 (7 ounce) package wild rice

▶ Saute pecan halves in melted butter in skillet.

▶ Prepare wild rice according to package directions and stir pecans into rice. Serve hot with chicken or pork. Serves 2 to 3.

Mushroom Rice

1 cup brown rice
2 bouillon cubes
1 (4 ounce) can sliced mushrooms, drained
⅓ cup slivered almonds
1 (8 ounce) carton sour cream

▶ Preheat oven to 350°.

▶ Prepare rice according to package directions and add bouillon.

▶ Add mushrooms, almonds and sour cream to rice and transfer to sprayed 3-quart baking dish. Cover and bake for 25 minutes. Serve 3 to 4.

Green Rice and Spinach

1 cup brown rice
1 (10 ounce) package frozen chopped spinach
1 onion, finely chopped
3 tablespoons butter
¾ cup shredded cheddar cheese, divided

▶ Preheat oven to 350°.

▶ Cook rice in large saucepan according to package directions.

▶ Punch holes in box of spinach and cook in microwave on HIGH for about 3 minutes.

▶ Set aside 3 tablespoons cheese for topping and add well drained spinach, onion, butter, remaining cheese and ¼ teaspoon salt to rice. (If rice mixture seems a little dry, add several tablespoons water.)

▶ Pour into sprayed 2-quart baking dish and sprinkle 3 tablespoons cheese on top. Bake for 25 minutes. Serves 2.

You don't have to measure water when cooking rice or grains. Just put your grain in a pot, shake grain down so it is even all around and then pour in enough water so that it covers the grain up to the first joint of your index finger.

1st Nutty Quinoa

2 cups quinoa, soaked
½ cup chopped red onion
2 tablespoons coconut oil
1 teaspoon ground cumin
¼ cup sliced almonds

▶ Soak quinoa at least 4 hours or overnight.

▶ Saute onion in coconut oil on medium-high heat. After 5 minutes throw in a little salt and pepper, cumin, and almonds. Saute for several minutes.

▶ Strain quinoa, pour into mixture and stir for a few more minutes. Lightly brown quinoa in saucepan, pour in just under 4 cups water and bring to a boil. Reduce to simmer and set timer for 20 minutes.

▶ Remove from heat and let stand in pot for additional 10 minutes while you set the table. This is the bomb! Serves 2 to 3.

TIP: *Quinoa is a tiny, bead-shaped grain that contains more protein than any other grain and it has all eight essential amino acids. This is a super grain.*

Red Rice

1 (16 ounce) package smoked sausage, sliced
2 (10 ounce) cans diced tomatoes and green chilies
3 cups chicken broth
2 teaspoons Creole seasoning
1½ cups long grain rice

▶ Saute sausage in large skillet until it is brown. Stir in tomatoes and green chilies, broth, and seasoning and bring to a boil.

▶ Stir in rice, cover and reduce heat. Simmer for 25 minutes, uncover and cook until liquid absorbs. Serves 3 to 4.

Italian-Style Rice and Beans

1 (16 ounce) package frozen chopped onions and bell peppers
2 tablespoons olive oil
1 (15 ounce) can Italian stewed tomatoes
1 (15 ounce) can great northern beans, drained
1 cup cooked rice

▶ Saute onions and bell peppers with oil in large saucepan. Add stewed tomatoes, beans, ½ cup water and rice and stir well.

▶ Cover and cook on medium-high heat for about 3 minutes. Uncover and continue cooking for additional 3 minutes or until rice is hot. Stir once or twice. Serves 3 to 4.

TIP: *Always try to use whole grain rice when you can.*

Super Supper Frittata

2 cups cooked white basmati rice
1 (10 ounce) box frozen green peas, thawed
1 cup cooked, cubed ham
Butter
8 large eggs, beaten
1 cup shredded pepper Jack cheese, divided
1 teaspoon dried thyme

▶ Preheat broiler.

▶ Heat rice, peas and ham with butter in large, heavy oven-proof skillet for 3 to 4 minutes or until mixture is thoroughly hot.

▶ In separate bowl, whisk eggs, three-fourths cheese, thyme and a little salt. Add to mixture in skillet and shake pan gently to distribute evenly. Cover and cook on medium heat, without stirring, until set on bottom and sides. Eggs will still be runny in center.

▶ Sprinkle remaining cheese over top. Place skillet in oven and broil for about 5 minutes or until frittata is firm in center. Serves 3 to 4.

TIP: *This can also be served as a main dish.*

Spanish Rice

6 tablespoons (¾ stick) butter, melted
1 onion, chopped
2 cups cooked rice
1 (10 ounce) can tomatoes and green chilies

▶ Preheat oven to 350°.

▶ Combine butter, onion, rice, tomatoes and green chilies, and a little salt in large bowl.

▶ Spoon mixture into sprayed 3-quart baking dish. Cover and bake for 30 minutes. Serves 3 to 4.

Tofu and Rice with Green Chilies

1 (14 ounce) package extra-firm tofu
1 (15 ounce) can diced tomatoes
1 (4 ounce) can chopped green chilies, drained
2 cups cooked brown rice
¼ cup sliced green onions
¼ cup chopped cilantro

▶ Blot tofu with paper towels to remove excess moisture. Cut into ½-inch cubes.

▶ Bring tomatoes and green chilies to a boil in non-stick 12-inch skillet over medium-high heat. Stir in rice and tofu, green onions and cilantro. Reduce heat to low, cover and simmer for 10 minutes. Serves 8.

TIP: *Serve with baked tortilla chips and your favorite salsa. This could also be served as a main dish.*

Remember, one of the secrets to the Healthy, Fast and Cheap™ lifestyle is cooking a large pot of whole grains once a week and including it in multiple meals throughout the week!

Basic Pasta Styles

Tube Pastas
- Elbow pasta – any variety of curved, tubular pastas
- Macaroni – tube shapes of different lengths about ½ inch wide
- Manicotti – large tubes used for filling; usually about 4 inches long and 1 inch wide
- Penne – diagonally cut tubes
- Rigatoni – large grooved macaroni

Ribbon Pastas
- Fettuccini or fettuccine – thin, flat egg noodles about ¼-inch wide
- Linguine – "little tongues"; narrow, flat noodles about ⅛-inch wide

Strands
- Spaghetti – "strings"; round, thin strands
- Capelli d'angelo – "angel hair"; long, extremely fine, delicate strands
- Lasagna or lasagne – long noodles about 2 to 3 inches wide
- Spaghettini – very thin spaghetti, but thicker than fettuccine
- Vermicelli – very long, thin strands

Spirals
- Cavatappi – "corkscrew"; short, thin spirals
- Fusilli – "little springs"; spirals about 1½ inches long

Shells and Patterns
- Conchiglie – "conch shells"; seashell-shaped pasta
- Farfalle – "butterflies"; bow-tie or butterfly shaped pasta

Stuffed Pastas
- Ravioli – square-shaped with filling
- Tortellini – small stuffed pasta
- Tortelloni – large tortellini

Pasta

Homemade Pesto

Everyone needs a basic pesto sauce for linguine or angel hair pasta. This basil pesto is a true classic and always good.

2 cups fresh basil leaves or Italian parsley
1 cup shredded fresh parmesan cheese
3 cloves garlic, peeled, minced
½ cup chopped pine nuts
½ cup extra-virgin olive oil

▶ Remove all stems or dried areas on basil leaves, wash and drain thoroughly. Pat dry with paper towels.

▶ Add parmesan, garlic and pine nuts to food processor and process until ingredients are coarsely chopped.

▶ Add basil to cheese mixture and process while pouring olive oil over ingredients. Process until basil is finely chopped, but not pureed.

▶ Add salt and course ground black pepper to taste and serve within 2 days. Serve with linguine or angel hair pasta. Serves 2 to 3.

Basil with Pasta

2½ cups small tube pasta
1 small onion, chopped
2 tablespoons olive oil
2½ tablespoons dried basil
1 cup shredded mozzarella cheese

▶ Cook pasta according to package directions. Saute onion with oil in skillet.

▶ Add basil, 1 teaspoon salt and ¼ teaspoon pepper; cook and stir for 1 minute.

▶ Drain pasta but leave about ½ cup water so pasta won't be too dry. Add to basil mixture. Remove from heat and stir in cheese just until it begins to melt. Serve immediately. Serves 2 to 3.

Artichoke Fettuccini

1 (12 ounce) package fettuccini
1 (10 ounce) box frozen spinach, thawed
1 (14 ounce) can water-packed artichoke hearts, drained, chopped
1 (16 ounce) jar alfredo sauce
2 heaping tablespoons crumbled blue cheese

▶ Cook fettuccini according to package directions. Drain, place in serving bowl and keep warm.

▶ Squeeze spinach between paper towels to completely remove excess moisture.

▶ Heat artichoke hearts, spinach and alfredo sauce in large saucepan and stir well. Spoon into bowl with fettuccini and toss. Sprinkle with blue cheese and serve hot. Serves 4.

TIP: Look for whole wheat pasta for the most nutritious dish.

Macaroni and Cheese

1 cup macaroni, divided
¼ cup (½ stick) butter, sliced
1½ cups shredded sharp cheddar, colby or Velveeta® cheese*
⅔ cup milk

▶ Preheat oven to 350°.

▶ Cook macaroni according to package directions and drain. Stir in butter and mix to melt. Put half macaroni in sprayed baking dish.

▶ Mix cheese, milk and a little salt and pepper in bowl and pour half over macaroni.

▶ Pour remaining macaroni into dish and cover with remaining cheese mixture. Bake until brown on top. Serves 2 to 4.

*TIP: Velveeta® is a processed food and not as healthy as other cheeses, but it melts better than most other cheeses and it's probably what your mother used. If you choose to eat it, use moderation.

Skillet Ravioli and Broccoli

1 (16 ounce) package refrigerated cheese ravioli
1 (16 ounce) package frozen broccoli florets, thawed
1 (16 ounce) carton marinara sauce
¾ cup shredded mozzarella cheese

▶ Cook ravioli in boiling water in large saucepan for 8 minutes or until tender. Drain ravioli and return to saucepan.

▶ Cook broccoli according to package directions and drain. Stirring gently, add broccoli and marinara sauce to ravioli in saucepan.

▶ Cook on medium heat, stirring often, just until mixture is thoroughly hot. Sprinkle with cheese, cover and cook for 1 minute until cheese melts. Serves 4.

Spinach Fettuccini

1 (12 ounce) package spinach fettuccini
1 (6 ounce) can tomato paste
½ cup whipping cream
½ cup (1 stick) butter

▶ Cook fettuccini according to package directions.

▶ Combine tomato paste, cream and butter in saucepan and cook until butter melts. Season with a little salt and pepper.

▶ Serve sauce over fettuccini. Serves 3 to 4.

The top five best foods include dark green leafy vegetables, papaya, avocado, cold water fish and blueberries.

A Word on Vegetables

It seems that some folks insist on eating vegetables in completely boring ways because they think vegetables are supposed to be "healthy". Well, the only way vegetables can be healthy is if they make their way to your mouth and on into your belly. In order for them to be in your digestive tract, they need to taste good. For them to taste good, you need to use fat, salt, condiments and seasonings on them. High quality fat not only helps your food taste good, it also helps in the following ways.

- Improves the assimilation of fat-soluble vitamins in vegetables
- Reduces cravings for fat from junk food
- Satisfies more completely

Don't hesitate to add olive oil, coconut oil, organic butter, high quality cold-pressed sesame oil, almond oil, macadamia nut oil or other cold-pressed oils. Go ahead and put on cheese and/or sauce, but do so in moderation. In our kitchen we keep a lazy susan with gomasio, hot sauce, Bragg Liquid Aminos, nutritional yeast, adobo, olive oil, pepper and salt, and whatever other condiments are turning us on.

Veggies

 ## My Suggestion for Cooking Veggies

Cook veggies by steaming or boiling them, but don't overdo it. Serve them up and then add fat and flavor by adding your favorite condiments. It's hard to go wrong with olive oil and tamari.

 ## One Vegetable Group You Can't Do Without: Greens!

There are two ways I recommend getting greens into your belly. You can simply buy frozen collard, mustard or spinach greens and drop them directly into a pot. Cook them for 10 minutes on medium heat and serve with a little butter for added flavor.

My favorite option, however, is roasted greens. If you haven't liked greens before, this will convert you! (See Roasted Kale on page 201 for directions.)

Asparagus Caesar

3 (15 ounce) cans asparagus spears, drained
¼ cup (½ stick) butter, melted
3 tablespoons lemon juice
½ cup grated parmesan cheese

▶ Preheat oven to 400°.

▶ Place asparagus in 2-quart baking dish. Drizzle on butter and lemon juice. Sprinkle cheese and bake for 15 to 20 minutes. Serves 4 to 6.

Oven-Baked Asparagus

1 bunch fresh asparagus, trimmed
2 tablespoons extra-virgin olive oil
2 tablespoons balsamic vinegar
⅓ cup freshly grated parmesan cheese

▶ Preheat oven to 400°.

▶ Arrange asparagus in single layer in shallow baking dish and drizzle olive oil over asparagus. Bake for about 10 minutes. To serve, sprinkle with a little salt and pepper, vinegar, and parmesan cheese. Serves 4.

Quick Asparagus

1 bunch fresh asparagus
2 tablespoons olive oil

▶ Preheat oven to 400°.

▶ Wash asparagus and dry with paper towels. Place in baking dish bowl and drizzle with olive oil.

▶ Roast for 5 to 10 minutes or until asparagus is tender-crisp.

▶ Slide asparagus onto serving plate and season with salt and pepper. Serves 4.

Crunchy Broccoli

2 (10 ounce) packages frozen broccoli florets
1 (8 ounce) can sliced water chestnuts, drained, chopped
½ cup (1 stick) butter, melted
1 teaspoon garlic powder
1 teaspoon onion powder

▶ Steam broccoli in saucepan for about 10 minutes or until just tender. It should not be mushy.

▶ Add water chestnuts and steam for additional 1 minute and remove from heat.

▶ Combine melted butter, garlic powder, onion powder and 1 teaspoon salt in bowl. Pour over cooked broccoli and serve hot. Serves 4 to 6.

TIP: For a tasty boost, add 1 tablespoon nutritional yeast.

Creamy Cabbage Bake

1 head cabbage, shredded
1 cup sour cream
2 tablespoons soy sauce
⅔ cup milk
1 (8 ounce) package shredded cheddar cheese

▶ Preheat oven to 325°.

▶ Place cabbage in sprayed 2-quart baking dish. Mix sour cream, soy sauce and 1 teaspoon salt with milk in bowl and pour over top of cabbage.

▶ Cover and bake for 30 minutes. Uncover, sprinkle with cheese and bake until cheese melts. Serves 4 to 6.

Scalloped Cabbage

2 small heads cabbage, cut up
1 (10 ounce) can cream of celery soup
1 cup shredded cheddar cheese
⅓ cup crumbled saltine crackers

▶ Preheat oven to 350°.

▶ Cut whole cabbages into quarters to easily remove thick white core. Place cut up cabbage in saucepan with 2 cups water and 1 teaspoon salt.

▶ Cook for 8 minutes and drain. Transfer cabbage to sprayed 2-quart baking dish.

▶ Combine celery soup, ½ cup water and cheddar cheese in saucepan on medium heat, whisk, stirring constantly, until mixture heats and cheese begins to melt.

▶ Pour mixture over cabbage and sprinkle with crumbled crackers. Bake for 20 minutes. Serves 4 to 6.

TIP: *Look for all-natural soups to get the most nutrition.*

Speedy Cabbage

1 head cabbage, shredded
2 tablespoons butter
3 tablespoons sour cream
½ teaspoon sugar

▶ Saute cabbage in butter and about 2 tablespoons water in saucepan until tender (about 3 to 4 minutes), stirring constantly.

▶ Stir in sour cream, about ½ teaspoon each of salt and pepper, and sugar. Serve hot. Serves 4 to 6.

Glazed Carrots

1 (16 ounce) package frozen baby carrots
¼ cup apple cider
¼ cup apple jelly
1½ teaspoons dijon-style mustard

▶ Place carrots and apple cider in saucepan and bring to a boil. Reduce heat. Cover and simmer for about 8 minutes or until carrots are tender.

▶ Remove cover and cook on medium heat until liquid evaporates. Stir in jelly and mustard. Cook until jelly melts and carrots glaze. Serves 4 to 5.

Tangy Carrot Coins

2 (15 ounce) cans sliced carrots
2 tablespoons butter
2 tablespoons brown sugar
1 tablespoon dijon-style mustard

▶ Place all ingredients in saucepan. Cook and stir over medium heat for about 2 minutes until hot. Serves 6 to 8.

Creamy Cauliflower

1 head cauliflower, broken into large florets
1 red bell pepper, seeded, chopped
1 small zucchini, chopped
1 (10 ounce) can cream of celery soup
⅓ cup milk

▶ Place cauliflower florets, red bell pepper and zucchini in saucepan with ¾ cup water and a little salt. Cover and cook on high heat for about 10 minutes or until cauliflower is tender. Drain.

▶ In smaller saucepan, combine soup and milk and heat, stirring until they mix well. Spoon cauliflower, bell pepper and zucchini into serving bowl and pour soup mixture over vegetables. Serves 4 to 6.

Atomic Salsa-Corn

1 (8 ounce) jar hot salsa
1 (16 ounce) package frozen whole kernel corn, thawed
¼ teaspoon garlic powder
½ cup grated Monterey Jack cheese

▶ Combine hot salsa, corn, garlic powder and ¼ cup water in saucepan.

▶ Cook on medium-low heat, stirring occasionally, for 6 minutes. Pour into serving bowl and sprinkle with cheese. Serves 4 to 5.

Corn au Gratin

2 (15 ounce) cans Mexicorn®, drained
1 (4 ounce) can sliced mushrooms, drained
1 (10 ounce) can cream of mushroom soup
1 cup shredded cheddar cheese

▶ Mix all ingredients in saucepan and heat slowly until cheese melts. Serve hot. Serves 6 to 8.

TIP: For a more nutritious dish, add 2 cups cooked amaranth.

Grilled Corn-on-the-Cob

Fresh corn-on-the-cob in husks
Butter

▶ Shuck each ear of corn by removing outer husks, but save husks.

▶ Remove all silk and spread butter all over corn. Season with salt and pepper and wrap corn in inner husks and large outer husks to hold butter. Tie closed with long pieces of outer husks.

▶ Place on grill and cook for 15 to 30 minutes or until corn is tender. Turn once or twice while cooking. Remove from grill and serve hot. Serve 1 per person.

Hot Corn Bake

3 (15 ounce) cans whole kernel corn, drained
1 (10 ounce) can cream of corn soup
1 cup salsa
1 (8 ounce) package shredded Mexican-cheese blend, divided

▶ Preheat oven to 350°.

▶ Combine corn, soup, salsa and half cheese in bowl and mix well.

▶ Pour into sprayed 3-quart baking dish and sprinkle remaining cheese on top. Bake for 20 to 30 minutes. Serves 6 to 8.

TIP: For a more nutritious dish, add 1 cup cooked quinoa.

Classic Baked Beans

2 (16 ounce) cans pork and beans, slightly drained
1 tablespoon Worcestershire sauce
½ onion, chopped
½ cup honey or maple syrup
3 dashes hot sauce
1 teaspoon mustard
1¼ cups tomato sauce
3 strips bacon

▶ Preheat oven to 350°

▶ Combine beans, Worcestershire sauce, onion, honey, hot sauce, mustard and tomato sauce in bowl and mix well.

▶ Pour into sprayed baking dish and place bacon strips over beans. Bake for 45 to 50 minutes. Serves 8.

The Green Bean Casserole

½ cup chopped onion
Butter
2 (14 ounce) cans French-cut green beans, drained
1 (5 ounce) can sliced water chestnuts, drained
1 (10 ounce) can cream of mushroom soup
2 cups shredded sharp cheddar cheese

▶ Preheat oven to 350°.

▶ Saute onion in butter, drain and set aside.

▶ Combine green beans and water chestnuts with mushroom soup in medium bowl.

▶ Pour green bean mixture into sprayed 9 x 13-inch baking dish and top with cheddar cheese.

▶ Bake for 15 minutes. Remove from oven and pour onion evenly over top of casserole. Bake for additional 15 to 20 minutes or until thoroughly hot and brown on top. Serves 6 to 8.

Green Beans and Almonds

2 (16 ounce) packages frozen french-cut green beans
2 tablespoons butter
2 (8 ounce) cans water chestnuts, chopped
½ cup slivered almonds, toasted

▶ Cook beans according to package directions.

▶ Drain, add butter and heat just until butter melts. Fold in water chestnuts. Place in serving dish and sprinkle almonds over top. Serves 6 to 8.

For veggies to taste good, you may want to put fat, salt, condiments and seasonings on them. High quality fat not only helps your food taste good, it also reduces cravings for fat from junk food, improves the assimilation of fat-soluble vitamins in the veggies and satisfies more completely.

Green Beans and Mushrooms

½ cup (1 stick) butter, divided
1 small onion, chopped
1 (8 ounce) carton fresh mushrooms, sliced
2 pounds fresh green beans, trimmed
¾ cup chicken broth

▶ Melt half butter in saucepan and saute onion and mushrooms and transfer to small bowl.

▶ In same saucepan, melt remaining butter and toss with green beans. Pour chicken broth over beans and bring to a boil; reduce heat, cover and simmer until liquid evaporates and green beans are tender-crisp. Stir in mushroom mixture and season with salt. Serves 6 to 8.

Parmesan Peas

2 (10 ounce) packages frozen green peas
3 tablespoons butter, melted
1 tablespoon lemon juice
⅓ cup grated parmesan cheese

▶ Microwave peas in 2 tablespoons water in microwave-safe bowl for 3 minutes.

▶ Rotate bowl and cook for additional 3 minutes. Stir in butter, lemon juice and parmesan. Serves 6 to 8.

 # Roasted Kale

1 bunch kale, washed, sliced
2 tablespoons coconut or olive oil
2 tablespoons tamari

▶ Preheat broiler.

▶ Remove stems from kale and toss with oil and tamari. Arrange on baking sheet and place in oven. After about 2 minutes toss and broil for a few more minutes.

▶ When it's done, you'll have a crisp, tasty and healthy accompaniment to any meal. Serves 2 to 4.

Homemade Mashed Potatoes

3 - 4 large baking potatoes
¼ cup milk
⅓ cup butter

▶ Peel or don't peel each potato and cut into 4 to 6 pieces. (Scrub potatoes thoroughly if you choose not to peel them.) Add potatoes to saucepan, cover with water and boil until tender. Drain water and pour potatoes into bowl. Cool and cut into small pieces.

▶ Beat potatoes in bowl until they blend, but are still a little lumpy. Add milk, butter, and 1 teaspoon each of salt and pepper. Whip potatoes until smooth and creamy. Serves 4 to 6.

Broccoli-Topped Potatoes

4 hot baked potatoes, halved
1 cup cooked, diced ham
1 (10 ounce) can cream of broccoli soup
½ cup shredded cheddar cheese

▶ Place hot baked potato halves on oven-safe plate. Carefully fluff up potatoes with fork. Top each potato with ham.

▶ Stir soup in can until smooth. Spoon soup over potatoes and top with cheese. Bake at 400° for 10 to 15 minutes. Serves 4.

Ham-It-Up Potatoes

4 large baking potatoes, baked
¼ cup (½ stick) butter
¼ cup sour cream
1 cup finely chopped leftover or deli ham
1 (10 ounce) package frozen broccoli florets, coarsely chopped
1 cup shredded sharp cheddar cheese

▶ Preheat oven to 400°.

▶ Slit potatoes down center, but not through to bottom. For each potato, use 1 tablespoon each of butter and sour cream.

▶ With fork, work in ¼ cup ham, one-fourth broccoli and ¼ cup cheese in each potato. Before serving, place potatoes on baking sheet and heat for 10 minutes. Serves 6 to 8.

Creamy Ranch Potatoes

4 medium russet potatoes, peeled, quartered
¼ cup (½ stick) butter
⅓ cup ranch salad dressing

▶ Boil potatoes in water in saucepan for about 15 minutes or until tender. Drain and beat potatoes with mixer until smooth.

▶ Add butter, ½ teaspoon salt and a little pepper and beat until butter melts. Gradually add salad dressing and beat until smooth. Spoon into serving bowl. Serves 3 to 4.

Potato Souffle

2⅔ cups cooked mashed potatoes
2 eggs, beaten
1 cup shredded cheddar cheese

▶ Preheat oven to 325°.

▶ Combine potatoes, eggs and cheese in bowl and stir until they blend well.

▶ Spoon mixture into lightly sprayed 2-quart dish. Bake for 25 minutes. Serves 4.

Rosemary New Potatoes

2 pounds small red (new) potatoes, halved
¼ cup olive oil
1 teaspoon dried rosemary

▶ Place potatoes in saucepan with about 1-inch of water and a little salt. Cover and cook on medium heat, turning occasionally, until tender (about 15 minutes).

▶ Drain and toss with olive oil, rosemary, 1 teaspoon salt and ample amount of pepper. Cover again to keep warm. Serves 6 to 8.

Baked Sweet Potatoes

4 sweet potatoes
¼ cup (½ stick) butter, melted

▶ Preheat oven to 350°.

▶ Coat sweet potatoes with butter or oil. Pierce skins with fork and bake for 1 hour. Serves 4.

TIP: *Use a baking sheet or aluminum foil under the rack to catch the drippings.*

Stir-Fry Squash-Onions

¼ cup extra-virgin olive oil
4 medium zucchini, sliced
3 medium yellow squash, sliced
2 green bell peppers, seeded, julienned
2 yellow onions, sliced, separated into rings

▶ Heat oil in skillet on medium heat and stir-fry zucchini, squash, bell peppers and onions for about 30 minutes.

▶ Toss several times to brown lightly. Season with 2 teaspoons each of salt and pepper and serve immediately. Serves 6 to 8.

Herbed Spinach

2 (16 ounce) packages frozen chopped spinach
1 (8 ounce) package cream cheese, softened
¼ cup (½ stick) butter, melted, divided
1 cup crushed whole grain crackers with herbs

▶ Preheat oven to 350°.

▶ Cook spinach according to package directions. Squeeze spinach between paper towels to completely remove excess moisture. Add cream cheese and half butter. Season with a little salt and pepper.

▶ Pour into sprayed baking dish. Spread herb cracker stuffing on top and drizzle with remaining butter. Bake for 25 minutes. Serves 4 to 6.

Wilted Spinach with Walnuts

2 (8 ounce) packages baby spinach, stemmed
1 teaspoon minced garlic
2 tablespoons olive oil
Seasoned salt
¼ cup walnut halves, toasted

▶ Saute spinach and garlic with hot oil in large skillet on medium-high heat for 6 minutes or until spinach wilts. Sprinkle a little seasoned salt over spinach and mix. Toss with toasted walnuts. Serves 4 to 5.

TIP: *To toast walnuts, bake at 300° for about 6 minutes.*

Walnut Zucchini

6 - 8 small zucchini, julienned
½ red bell pepper, seeded, julienned
¼ cup (½ stick) butter
1 cup chopped walnuts

▶ Saute zucchini and bell pepper with butter in skillet until tender. Shake pan and toss zucchini to cook evenly. Pour off any excess butter.

▶ Add chopped walnuts and a little salt and pepper. When mixture is hot, serve immediately. Serves 4 to 6.

Buttered Vegetables

½ cup (1 stick) butter
2 yellow squash, sliced
1 (16 ounce) package broccoli florets
1 (10 ounce) package frozen corn

▶ Melt butter in large skillet and combine all vegetables. Saute vegetables for about 10 to 15 minutes or until tender-crisp. Serves 4 to 5.

1st Grilled Vegetables

Lots of vegetables can be grilled and an open fire brings out lots of flavor. Choose your favorites.

Grape tomatoes
Roma tomatoes
Button mushrooms
Bell pepper (green, yellow and red), seeded, quartered
Zucchini, sliced lengthwise
Yellow squash, sliced lengthwise
Texas SuperSweet 1015 or Vidalia® onions, peeled, quartered
Jalapenos, seeded, veined
Portobello mushrooms
Asparagus
Eggplant
Poblano peppers
Olive oil

▶ Lightly coat vegetables with olive oil and a little salt and pepper. Skewer and alternate small vegetables like tomatoes and button mushrooms and place larger vegetables directly on grill.

▶ Skewers with 1 slice onion, 1 slice green bell pepper, 1 to 2 grape tomatoes, 1 button mushroom, 1 slice yellow bell pepper, another onion slice, etc., make a beautiful vegetable medley.

▶ Place over medium-low heat and cook long enough for veggies to be tender-crisp. Make sure grill marks show.

Stay the Course

Chicken Main Dishes
Beef Main Dishes
Pork Main Dishes
Seafood Main Dishes

Leaving Home Cookbook and Survival Guide

Stay the Course Contents

Chicken Main Dishes

 ## 1st Roast Chicken

This is easy, inexpensive and you can use it to make a great soup when you are finished. Now are you ready for how easy this is?

1 (2½ - 3 pound) chicken

▶ Wash whole chicken, pat it dry, put it in baking pan, and dust with salt and pepper. Cover and bake at 350° for 1 hour 30 minutes.

▶ Remove cover and bake for additional 15 minutes. Remove chicken when the skin is brown and crispy.

TIP: *Many recommend cooking the chicken with the breast side up, but I say just get it in the oven and cook it any way you can.*

For the experienced cook, this may not be the ideal way to cook a chicken, but this achieves several objectives: it is simple, fast and it assures that your bird cooks completely. You don't have to mess around with a meat thermometer. The chicken is done when juices next to bone run clear.

One tip you can't pass up is to stick a piece of fruit or vegetable (apple, cut lemon, some carrot chunks, etc.) inside the chicken cavity to make the meat really most and tasty.

The general rule for roasting a chicken is to cook it for 20 minutes per pound. When you cover the roasting pan, it doesn't dry out. When you remove the lid, the outside browns and looks more appealing.

My Favorite Leftover Chicken Recipe

Leftover chicken
1 (16 ounce) package frozen spinach, thawed
1 (5.6 ounce) can coconut milk
Cumin
Coriander

▶ Take a handful of chicken, chop it up and throw it in a pot with spinach. Add coconut milk, toss in some pepper, cumin, coriander and salt and cook for 5 to 10 minutes. Serves 2 to 4.

Beer-in-the-Rear Chicken

1 (2½ - 3 pound) chicken
Olive oil
Garlic powder
Onion, apple or celery slices
1 (12 ounce) can light beer

▶ Preheat oven to 350°.

▶ Wash chicken inside and out and dry with paper towel.

▶ Rub chicken with olive oil and sprinkle garlic powder and a little salt and pepper inside and out. Place slice of onion, apple or celery in cavity of chicken.

▶ Open can of bear and poke several more holes in top. Insert can of beer upright into cavity of chicken and place upright chicken in shallow baking pan.

▶ Place chicken in oven and bake for 1 hour 20 minutes or until juices run clear or grill, covered, over medium hot fire and cook until juices run clear. Serves 4.

Broccoli-Rice Chicken

1¼ cups converted rice
2 pounds boneless, skinless chicken breast halves
Dried parsley
1 all natural bouillon cube
1 (14 ounce) can chicken broth
¼ cup (½ stick) butter

▶ Place rice in slow cooker. Slice chicken and put over rice. Sprinkle with parsley and a little pepper.

▶ Combine bouillon and chicken broth and 1 cup water in saucepan. Heat just enough to mix well. Pour over chicken and rice. Cover and cook on LOW for 6 to 8 hours. Serves 4 to 6.

TIP: *This is a great recipe to try quinoa, a bead-like grain that is a great, nutritious substitute for rice.*

Wild Rice and Chicken

1 (6 ounce) package long grain-wild rice mix
4 boneless, skinless chicken breast halves
½ cup (1 stick) butter, divided
1 large green bell pepper, seeded, chopped

▶ Prepare rice according to package directions.

▶ Cook chicken in ¼ cup butter in large skillet. Make sure each chicken breast browns on both sides and juices run clear. Remove chicken and keep warm.

▶ Add remaining butter to pan drippings and saute bell pepper until tender. Add to rice. Serve with cooked chicken breasts. Serves 4.

Chicken-Broccoli Casserole

1 (10 ounce) can cream of chicken soup
⅔ cup milk
1 cup shredded mozzarella cheese
1 cup cooked brown rice
2 cups cooked, cubed chicken
1 (10 ounce) package frozen broccoli florets, thawed

▶ Heat soup with milk and cheese in saucepan over medium heat.

▶ Stir in brown rice and mix well. Add chicken and broccoli and heat thoroughly; stir occasionally.

▶ Transfer to serving dish and serve immediately. Serves 4 to 6.

TIP: *For a healthier dish, replace cream of chicken soup with 1 cup half-and-half cream and 2 tablespoons all natural veggie soup bouillon or cubes.*

Cheesy Crusted Chicken

¾ cup mayonnaise (not light)
½ cup grated parmesan cheese
8 boneless chicken thighs and legs
1 cup Italian seasoned breadcrumbs

▶ Preheat oven to 400°.

▶ Combine mayonnaise and parmesan cheese in bowl. Place chicken pieces on wax paper and spread mayonnaise-cheese mixture over chicken. Sprinkle all sides heavily with dry breadcrumbs.

▶ Place chicken on large sprayed baking pan. Make sure pieces do not touch. Bake for 20 minutes or until juices runs clear. Serves 6 to 8.

TIP: *You can use crushed crackers instead of Italian breadcrumbs. Just add a little oregano, basil and garlic powder.*

Teriyaki Wingettes

2½ pounds chicken wingettes
1 onion, chopped
1 cup soy sauce
½ cup unrefined brown sugar or 1 cup packed brown sugar
1 teaspoon minced garlic

▶ Rinse chicken and pat dry. Place chicken wingettes on broiler pan and broil for about 10 minutes on both sides. Transfer wingettes to large slow cooker.

▶ Combine onion, soy sauce, brown sugar and garlic in bowl. Spoon sauce over wingettes.

▶ Cook on HIGH for 2 hours. Stir wingettes once during cooking to coat chicken evenly with sauce. Serves 8 to 10.

Chicken Quesadillas

3 boneless, skinless chicken breast halves, cubed
⅔ cup chunky salsa
1 cup shredded sharp cheddar cheese
10 flour tortillas

▶ Preheat oven to 400°.

▶ Cook chicken in skillet and stir often until juices evaporate. Add salsa and heat thoroughly.

▶ Spread about ⅓ cup chicken mixture and cheese on half tortilla to within ½ inch of edge. Moisten edge with water, fold over and seal. Place tortillas on 2 baking sheets. Bake for 5 to 6 minutes. Serves 4.

Chile Pepper Chicken

5 boneless, skinless chicken breast halves
8 - 10 crackers, crushed
1 (4 ounce) can chopped green chilies
Chunky salsa

▶ Preheat oven to 375°.

▶ Sprinkle salt and pepper on chicken and coat with crushed
crackers. Place in sprayed 9 x 13-inch baking dish. Bake for
25 minutes.

▶ Remove from oven, spread green chilies over chicken breasts and
bake for 5 minutes. Serve with salsa over each chicken breast.
Serves 4 to 6.

Chicken Taco Pie

1½ pounds boneless, skinless chicken breast halves
Olive oil
1 (1 ounce) packet taco seasoning mix
2 green bell peppers, finely chopped
1½ cups shredded Mexican 3-cheese blend
1 (8 ounce) package corn muffin mix
1 egg
⅓ cup milk

▶ Preheat oven to 400°.

▶ Cut chicken into 1-inch chunks, cook with a little oil in large
skillet on medium-high heat for about 10 minutes and drain.

▶ Stir in taco seasoning, bell peppers and ¾ cup water. Reduce heat
and simmer, stirring several times, for additional 10 minutes.
Spoon into sprayed 9-inch deep-dish pie pan and sprinkle
with cheese.

▶ Prepare corn muffin mix with egg and milk in bowl and mix
well. Spoon over top of pie and bake for 20 minutes or until top
is golden brown. Let stand for about 5 minutes before serving.
Serves 4.

TIP: *It's always best to use all natural ingredients, i.e., all natural corn
muffin mix.*

Grilled Chicken Fajitas

Marinade:

1 cup salsa
1 cup Italian vinaigrette
2 tablespoons lemon juice
2 tablespoons chopped green onions
1 teaspoon garlic powder

Chicken:

6 - 8 boneless, skinless chicken breast halves
Flour tortillas

Fillings for Fajitas:

Salsa
Guacamole
Grilled onions
Chopped tomatoes
Shredded cheese
Sour cream

▶ Combine all marinade ingredients and 1 teaspoon pepper in bowl and mix well.

▶ Remove any fat from meat, wipe dry with paper towels and place meat in shallow baking dish.

▶ Pour marinade over meat and marinate overnight or for at least 6 hours in refrigerator.

▶ Drain and discard liquid and grill over medium hot heat.

▶ Cut meat diagonally. Place a few strips on warmed flour tortilla, select fillings and roll to eat. Serves 6 to 8.

TIP: *Check out Healthy, Fast and Cheap™ Vinaigrette on page 154. Also, Easy Gringo Guacamole on page 51.*

Easy Chicken Parmesan

4 - 6 boneless, skinless chicken breast halves
⅓ cup (⅔ stick) butter, melted
1 cup grated parmesan cheese

▶ Preheat oven to 325°.

▶ Roll chicken in melted butter, then in parmesan cheese until pieces coat well.

▶ Place chicken in sprayed baking pan and drizzle a little extra butter over each piece. Bake for 45 to 50 minutes or until tender. Serves 4 to 6.

Chicken-Noodle Casserole

1 (8 ounce) package linguine pasta, divided
1 (10 ounce) can cream of chicken soup
½ cup half-and-half cream
1 cup shredded cheddar cheese
3 cups cooked, diced chicken
1 cup diced celery
1 cup slivered almonds, toasted, divided
1 cup seasoned breadcrumbs or crushed crackers

▶ Preheat oven to 375°.

▶ Cook pasta according to package directions and drain. Place half pasta in each of 2 small, sprayed baking dishes or 1 large baking dish. Combine soup, half-and-half cream and ¼ teaspoon salt in medium saucepan and heat, stirring constantly.

▶ Add cheese and stir until it melts. Add chicken, celery and half almonds and stir to mix well. Pour mixture over pasta in baking dishes. Top with remaining almonds and breadcrumbs. Bake for about 20 to 25 minutes until thoroughly hot. Serves 4.

TIP: If you make 2 casseroles, eat one and freeze the other after it cools.

Quick Chicken Supper

1 (16 ounce) package frozen broccoli florets, thawed
1¾ cup milk
⅔ cup mayonnaise
1 cup shredded cheddar cheese
3 cups cooked, cubed chicken
2 cups crushed cheese crackers

▶ Preheat oven to 375°.

▶ Combine broccoli, coconut milk, mayonnaise, cheese and chicken in large bowl and mix well. Pour into sprayed 3-quart baking dish, cover and bake for 20 minutes.

▶ Uncover, sprinkle crackers over casserole and bake for additional 10 minutes. Serves 4 to 6.

TIP: *Great spices for this dish include garlic powder, parsley and sea salt. If you have them on hand, you may want to try them. For a healthier touch, use coconut milk instead of regular milk.*

Chicken a la Orange

1 (11 ounce) can mandarin oranges, drained
1 (6 ounce) can frozen orange juice concentrate
1 tablespoon lemon juice
1 tablespoon cornstarch
4 boneless, skinless chicken breast halves
1 tablespoon seasoned salt
2 tablespoons butter

▶ Combine oranges, orange juice concentrate, lemon juice, ⅔ cup water and cornstarch in saucepan. Cook on medium heat, stirring constantly until mixture thickens. Set aside.

▶ Sprinkle chicken breasts with seasoned salt and place in skillet with butter. Cook for about 7 minutes on each side until brown.

▶ Lower heat and spoon orange juice mixture over chicken, cover and simmer for about 20 minutes. Add a little water if sauce gets too thick. Serves 4.

Favorite Chicken

6 boneless, skinless chicken breast halves
Olive oil
1 (16 ounce) jar thick-and-chunky hot salsa
½ cup applesauce
¼ cup honey
1 tablespoon dijon-style mustard
Brown rice, cooked

▶ Preheat oven to 350°.

▶ Brown chicken breasts with a little oil in large skillet and place in sprayed 9 x 13-inch baking dish.

▶ Combine salsa, applesauce, honey, mustard and ½ teaspoon salt in bowl and pour over chicken. Cover and bake for 35 minutes. Serve over brown rice. Serves 6.

Honey-Roasted Chicken

3 tablespoons soy sauce
3 tablespoons honey
2½ cups crushed wheat cereal
½ cup very finely minced walnuts
5 - 6 boneless, skinless chicken breast halves

▶ Preheat oven to 400°.

▶ Combine soy sauce and honey in shallow bowl and set aside. In separate shallow bowl, combine cereal and walnuts.

▶ Dip both sides of each chicken breast in soy sauce-honey mixture and dredge in cereal-walnut mixture. Place each piece on sprayed foil-lined baking sheet. Bake for 25 minutes (about 35 minutes if breasts are very large). Serves 6 to 8.

Parmesan Chicken

1 (1 ounce) package Italian salad dressing mix
½ cup grated parmesan cheese
¼ cup flour
¾ teaspoon garlic powder
5 boneless, skinless chicken breast halves

▶ Preheat oven to 375°.

▶ Combine salad dressing mix, cheese, flour and garlic powder in
shallow bowl. Moisten chicken with a little water and coat with
cheese mixture.

▶ Place in sprayed 9 x 13-inch baking pan. Bake for 25 minutes or
until chicken is light brown and cooks thoroughly. Serves 4 to 6.

TIP: *Instead of using Italian salad dressing mix, you could make your
own Italian spice mix with ½ teaspoon each of garlic powder,
oregano, pepper, paprika, celery salt and unrefined sugar.*

Tempting Chicken

3 boneless, skinless chicken breast halves
3 boneless, skinless chicken thighs
Olive oil
1 (10 ounce) can Italian tomato sauce
½ cup whipping cream
1 (10 ounce) can tomato bisque soup

▶ Preheat oven to 350°.

▶ Brown chicken pieces in little oil in large skillet. Place in sprayed
9 x 13-inch baking pan.

▶ Combine tomato sauce, cream, tomato bisque soup and ½ cup
water in bowl and pour over chicken. Cover and bake for about
20 minutes; uncover chicken and bake for additional 15 minutes.
Serves 4 to 6.

Chicken Stir-Fry

1 pound chicken tenders, cut in half lengthwise
2 tablespoons cornstarch
Olive oil
1 (16 ounce) package frozen broccoli, cauliflower and
      carrot medley, thawed
1 (10 ounce) package sugar snap peas
1 tablespoon chopped ginger
1 tablespoon minced garlic
¼ cup chopped green onions
⅔ cup soy sauce

▶ Place chicken tenders, cornstarch and a little salt and pepper in large resealable plastic bag, seal and shake to coat chicken. Stir-fry chicken with oil in large skillet on medium-high heat for about 10 minutes or until juices run clear. Transfer to plate.

▶ In same skillet with a little oil, add vegetables, ginger, garlic and green onions and cook for about 3 minutes. Cook until vegetables are tender-crisp; then add soy sauce.

▶ Add chicken to vegetable mixture and toss to mix. Serves 4.

Tasty Skillet Chicken

5 large boneless, skinless chicken breast halves, cut in strips
Olive oil
2 green bell peppers, seeded, julienned
2 small yellow squash, seeded, julienned
1 (16 ounce) bottle thick-and-chunky salsa
Rice, cooked

▶ Saute chicken with a little oil in large skillet for about 5 minutes. Add bell peppers and squash and cook for additional 5 minutes or until peppers are tender-crisp.

▶ Stir in salsa and bring to a boil; lower heat and simmer for 10 minutes. Serve over rice. Serves 4 to 6.

Baked Asian Veggies and Chicken

3 cups cooked, cubed chicken
1¾ cup milk
2 (16 ounce) package Asian vegetables, drained
1 (8 ounce) can sliced water chestnuts, drained
1 (16 ounce) package frozen seasoning blend (onions
      and bell peppers)
½ teaspoon hot sauce
¼ cup (½ stick) butter, melted
1 cup cooked brown rice

► Preheat oven to 350°.

► Combine chicken, milk, vegetables, water chestnuts, onions and bell peppers, and hot sauce in large bowl. Transfer into sprayed 9 x 13-inch baking dish. Combine butter and rice in bowl and sprinkle over top and bake for 30 minutes. Serves 3 to 4.

TIP: *Use coconut milk instead of regular milk for a healthier dish.*

Chicken Dijon

6 boneless, skinless chicken breast halves
¼ cup dijon-style mustard
2 cups finely crumbled seasoned breadcrumbs

► Preheat oven to 350°.

► Place chicken breasts in sprayed baking dish and bake for 20 minutes.

► Remove from heat and generously spread mustard on both sides of chicken. Coat with breadcrumbs and return to baking dish and bake for 1 hour or until juices run clear. Serves 6 to 8.

TIP: *The mustard gives chicken a tangy flavor and makes it moist. Don't overcook.*

Turkey Spaghetti

2 pounds ground turkey
2 (10 ounce) cans tomato bisque soup
1 (14 ounce) can chicken broth
2 (7 ounce) boxes ready-cut spaghetti, cooked, drained
1 (15 ounce) can whole kernel corn, drained
1 (4 ounce) can sliced mushrooms, drained

▶ Cook ground turkey in non-stick skillet and season with a little salt and pepper. Place cooked turkey in 5 to 6-quart slow cooker. Add in soup, broth, spaghetti, corn and mushrooms and stir to blend.

▶ Cover and cook on LOW for 5 to 7 hours or on HIGH for 3 hours. Serves 4 to 6.

Beef Main Dishes

Asian Beef-Noodles

1¼ pounds lean ground beef
1 teaspoon minced garlic
1 teaspoon minced ginger
1 (16 ounce) package frozen Oriental stir-fry vegetable mixture
1 (6 ounce) package rice noodles
3 tablespoons thinly sliced green onions
2 tablespoons soy sauce

▶ Brown ground beef in large skillet and drain. Add ½ cup water, garlic and ginger, and a little salt and pepper. Simmer for 10 minutes and transfer to separate bowl.

▶ In same skillet, combine 2 cups water, vegetables and noodles, and bring to a boil. Cover and cook for 3 minutes or until noodles are tender; stir occasionally. Return beef to skillet and stir in green onions and soy sauce. Serve right from skillet. Serves 3 to 4.

Beef Patties in Creamy Onion Sauce

1½ pounds lean ground beef
⅓ cup salsa
⅓ cup buttery cracker crumbs
1 (10 ounce) can cream of onion soup
Fettuccini pasta, cooked

▶ Combine beef, salsa and cracker crumbs in bowl and form into 5 to 6 patties. Brown in skillet and reduce heat. Add ¼ cup water and cook for 15 minutes.

▶ Combine onion soup and ½ cup water or milk in saucepan, heat and mix. Pour over beef patties. Serve over pasta. Serves 3 to 4.

TIP: *For the healthiest pasta, look for whole wheat.*

Beef Picante Skillet

1 pound lean ground beef
1 (10 ounce) can tomato soup
1 cup chunky salsa
6 (6 inch) flour tortillas, cut into 1-inch pieces
1¼ cups shredded cheddar cheese, divided

▶ Brown beef in skillet and drain. Add soup, salsa, ¾ cup water, tortilla pieces, ½ teaspoon salt and half of cheese.

▶ Heat to a boil, cover and cook over low heat for 5 minutes. Top with remaining cheese and serve right from skillet. Serves 3 to 4.

Beef Tacos

2 pounds lean ground beef
2 (1 ounce) packets taco seasoning
1 (8 ounce) can tomato sauce
24 taco shells
Shredded lettuce
Finely chopped ripe tomato, drained
Shredded longhorn cheese

▶ Brown meat in skillet, add taco seasoning and tomato sauce. Fill taco shells as desired with beef, lettuce, tomato and cheese. Serves 8 to 10.

Soft Beef Tacos

1 pound lean ground beef
1 tablespoon chili powder
1 small onion, chopped, divided
6 - 8 corn tortillas
1 large tomato, chopped
1 (12 ounce) package shredded cheddar cheese, divided

▶ Preheat oven to 350°.

▶ Brown ground beef in skillet, add chili powder and 1 tablespoon salt and cook for about 5 minutes.

▶ Put several tablespoons of meat and 1 teaspoon onion in middle of each tortilla, roll and place side by side in sprayed 10 x 15-inch baking dish.

▶ Combine tomato and remaining onion in bowl and sprinkle evenly over rolled tortillas.

▶ Spread cheese over top of tomatoes and bake for 10 to 15 minutes or until cheese melts. Serves 3 to 4.

TIP: If you don't want to heat them in the oven, put all the ingredients on the tortilla, roll and eat.

Bueno Taco Casserole

2 pounds lean ground beef
1½ cups taco sauce
4 cups fried rice
1 (8 ounce) package shredded Mexican 4-cheese blend, divided

▶ Preheat oven to 350°.

▶ Brown ground beef in skillet and drain. Add taco sauce, fried rice and half cheese.

▶ Spoon into sprayed 3-quart baking dish. Cover and bake for 35 minutes. Uncover and sprinkle remaining cheese on top and return to oven for 5 minutes. Serves 6 to 8.

TIP: To make fried rice, saute diced onion, diced bell pepper and diced celery in 2 tablespoons butter. As veggies start to brown, add cooked rice and cook on medium heat for about 5 minutes.

Beef Burritos

A flour tortilla and some refried beans make this a nice little sandwich — Texas-style.

1 pound lean ground beef
1 tablespoon chili powder
2 onions, chopped
1 (15 ounce) can refried beans
4 - 6 flour tortillas, warmed
1 (8 ounce) package shredded Mexican 4-cheese blend
1 tomato, chopped
Salsa

▶ Brown ground beef with 1 teaspoon salt and chili powder in heavy skillet.

▶ Drain grease, add onions and cook until onions are translucent.

▶ Heat refried beans in saucepan. Spread several tablespoons refried beans on warmed flour tortilla.

▶ Add ground beef, cheese and tomato and roll, folding up both ends. Serve with salsa. Serves 4 to 6.

TIP: If you make A Basic Pot of Beans on page 158, this is a great meal to make with leftover beans and it's cheap.

Easy Salisbury Steak

1¼ pounds lean ground beef
½ cup flour
1 egg
1 (10 ounce) can beef gravy
Rice or quinoa, cooked

▶ Preheat oven to 350°.

▶ Combine beef, flour and egg in large bowl. Add a little salt and pepper and mix well. Shape into 5 patties and place in shallow 7 x 11-inch baking dish.

▶ Bake for 20 minutes and drain off any fat. Pour beef gravy over patties. Bake for additional 20 minutes. Serve with rice or quinoa. Serves 4 to 6.

Meatloaf

1½ pounds lean ground beef
1 egg
½ cup milk
1 cup breadcrumbs
½ cup chopped onion
1 (6 ounce) can tomato paste

▶ Preheat oven to 325°.

▶ Mix ground beef, 1 teaspoon salt, egg, milk, breadcrumbs, onion
and tomato paste in large bowl. Form meat mixture into loaf.
Place in sprayed 9 x 9-inch baking dish (or whatever you have)
and bake for 50 to 60 minutes. Serves 4 to 6.

Tomato Sauce

2 tablespoons olive oil
¾ cup tomato paste
2½ cups canned chopped stewed tomatoes
1 teaspoon honey
5 tablespoons butter

▶ Heat oil in heavy saucepan over medium heat and stir in tomato
paste, stewed tomatoes, honey and butter. Simmer for about
30 minutes. Add a little salt and pepper and stir. Pour over
meatloaf during last 15 minutes of cooking or serve on the side.

The highest form of discipline in eating is not will power.
It's paying attention to how you respond to what you eat.
How will you feel the next time you eat that food? If you
eat a pastry in the morning for breakfast, how do you
feel afterwards? How about in an hour? In 2 hours?

Spaghetti and Meatballs

Meatballs:

1 pound lean ground round
2 eggs
1 cup shredded mozzarella cheese
¾ cup dry French breadcrumbs
1 onion, chopped
1 clove garlic, pressed
¼ cup milk
2 teaspoons ketchup
Olive oil

▶ Combine ground meat, eggs, cheese, breadcrumbs, onion, garlic, milk, ketchup, and a little salt and pepper in bowl and shape into balls.

▶ Brown meatballs in olive oil in skillet, drain on paper towel and set aside. Serves 3 to 4.

Sauce:

1 clove garlic, pressed
1 teaspoon olive oil
1 (6 ounce) can tomato paste
1½ teaspoons minced sweet basil
1½ teaspoons oregano
1 (12 ounce) box whole wheat spaghetti, cooked

▶ Saute garlic in olive oil in heavy saucepan until soft and clear. Add tomato paste, 3 cups water, basil, oregano, and a little salt and pepper and mix well.

▶ Add browned meatballs and simmer for 1 one hour or until sauce thickens. Serve over spaghetti.

Make-Believe Lasagna

1 pound lean ground beef
1 onion, chopped
½ teaspoon garlic powder
1 (18 ounce) can spaghetti sauce
½ teaspoon oregano
6 - 8 lasagna noodles, divided
1 (12 ounce) carton cottage cheese, divided
½ cup grated parmesan cheese, divided
1 (12 ounce) package shredded mozzarella cheese, divided

▶ Brown ground beef and onion in large skillet. Add garlic powder, spaghetti sauce and oregano. Cook just until thoroughly warm.

▶ Spoon layer of meat sauce in sprayed, oval slow cooker. Add layer of half lasagna noodles. (Break to fit slow cooker.)

▶ Top with layer of half remaining meat sauce, half cottage cheese, half parmesan cheese and half mozzarella cheese.

▶ Add layers of lasagna noodles, remaining meat sauce, cottage cheese, parmesan cheese and mozzarella cheese.

▶ Cover and cook on LOW for 6 to 8 hours. Serves 4 to 6.

Overnight Brisket

2 tablespoons liquid smoke
1 (3 - 4 pound) trimmed brisket
Garlic powder

▶ Rub 2 tablespoons liquid smoke on sides of brisket and sprinkle with garlic powder. Wrap tightly in foil and refrigerate overnight.

▶ When ready to bake, preheat oven to 325°.

▶ Sprinkle with more garlic powder and rewrap in foil. Bake in 9 x 13-inch dish for 5 hours. Refrigerate overnight again.

▶ Next day, cut thin slices across the grain. Serves 8 to 10.

TIP: *When you serve this as leftovers, pour barbecue sauce over it and reheat.*

Pot Roast and Gravy

4 - 5 round boneless rump or chuck roast
Garlic powder
6 medium potatoes, peeled, quartered
8 carrots, peeled, quartered
3 onions, peeled, quartered

▶ Preheat oven to 350°.

▶ Set roast in roasting pan and sprinkle liberally with salt, pepper and garlic powder. Add 1 cup water.

▶ Roast for about 3 hours or until it is fork-tender.

▶ Add potatoes, carrots and onions. Cook for additional 35 to 40 minutes or until vegetables are tender. Place roast on platter and arrange potatoes, carrots and onion around it. Serves 10 to 12.

Gravy:

3 tablespoons cornstarch

▶ Combine cornstarch and ¾ cup water in bowl and add to juices left in roasting pan.

▶ Add ½ teaspoon salt, cook on high on stove and stir constantly until gravy thickens. Serve with roast.

Easy Favorite Flank Steak

1 (2 pound) beef flank steak
⅓ cup teriyaki sauce
⅓ cup Worcestershire sauce

▶ Score flank steak with sharp knife and place in glass baking dish. Combine teriyaki and Worcestershire sauces in bowl and pour marinade over steak. Marinate steak in refrigerator for 2 to 4 hours. Turn steak several times.

▶ Remove steak from marinade (discard marinade) and broil or grill to desired doneness. Cook slowly to keep meat tender. Turn with tongs and broil other side.

▶ Let steak stand for 10 minutes before slicing. Slice diagonally across grain into thin strips. Serves 6 to 8.

TIP: *The cut to buy for beef fajitas is skirt steak or flank steak.*

Chicken-Fried Steak and Cream Gravy

½ cup milk
1 egg
¾ cup flour
1 (1½ pound) round steak, tenderized*
Olive oil

▶ Beat milk and egg in small bowl. In separate small flat bowl, mix flour, ½ teaspoon salt and ¼ teaspoon pepper.

▶ Cut tenderized round steak into 4 to 6 serving-size pieces. Coat each cutlet with seasoned flour, dip in milk-egg mixture and coat with seasoned flour again. Press flour into steak during last coating. (If you run out of flour, make more.)

▶ Pour about ¼ inch oil into skillet and heat. When oil sizzles, carefully lay each steak in skillet. Cook on each side until golden brown. Drain on paper towel. Serves 4.

Cream Gravy:

¼ cup (½ stick) butter
⅓ cup flour
3¼ cups milk

▶ Drain all drippings except 1 tablespoon from skillet. Add butter, flour, and ½ teaspoon each of salt and pepper.

▶ Over medium heat add in milk slowly, stirring constantly, until gravy thickens. Cook until heated thoroughly and serve immediately.

*TIP: *When you buy the round steak, ask the butcher to tenderize it or look for some that has already been tenderized. It will have tracks on it and look like an army tank ran over it. If you're not sure, you can always ask.*

Mock Filet Mignon

2 pounds ground round steak
1 (1 ounce) package onion soup mix
6 bacon slices

▶ Preheat oven to 450°.

▶ Combine ground round and soup mix in bowl. Shape into
6 thick patties and wrap slice of bacon around each. Secure
with toothpicks.

▶ Place in 9 x 13-inch dish and bake for 15 to 20 minutes or broil on
each side. Turn with spatula. Serves 6.

Pepper Steak

1 (1¼ pound) round steak, cut in strips
Seasoned salt
1 (16 ounce) package frozen bell pepper and onion strips, thawed
Rice, cooked

▶ Sprinkle steak with seasoned salt.

▶ Brown steak strips in sprayed large skillet, reduce heat and cook
over low heat for 10 minutes or until no longer pink. Remove
steak from skillet and set aside.

▶ In same skillet, add vegetables and ½ cup water and simmer for
5 minutes or until all liquid cooks out. Turn heat to medium-low
and stir in steak. Serve over rice. Serves 3 to 4.

*The top five worst foods include hydrogenated
oils, sugar (corn syrup, sucrose, dextrose, fructose),
white flour, refined salt and fast foods.*

Thai Beef, Noodles and Veggies

2 (4.4 ounce) packages Thai sesame noodles
1 pound round steak, cut in strips
Extra-virgin olive oil or canola oil
1 (16 ounce) package frozen stir-fry vegetables, thawed
½ cup chopped peanuts

▶ Cook noodles according to package directions, remove from heat and cover. Season steak strips with a little salt and pepper.

▶ Brown half steak strips in a little oil in skillet and cook slowly over low heat for about 5 minutes. Remove from skillet and drain on paper towel. Add remaining strips, brown in skillet with a little oil and cook slowly over low heat for about 5 minutes. Remove from skillet and drain on paper towel.

▶ In same skillet, place vegetables and ½ cup water, cover and cook for 5 minutes or until tender-crisp. Remove from heat, add steak strips and toss to mix. To serve, sprinkle with chopped peanuts. Serves 3 to 4.

TIP: *The key to cooking the steak is to cut thin strips and cook it slowly over low heat.*

Broiled Steak

1 (1 - 2 inch) thick sirloin, porterhouse or T-bone steak
Garlic salt
Worcestershire sauce

▶ Season steak with garlic salt, salt and pepper, and a little Worcestershire sauce on both sides. Allow steak to reach room temperature.

▶ Preheat broiler.

▶ Spray baking pan and place steak in center. Put oven rack about 4 to 5 inches from broiler and cook for about 3 to 5 minutes on each side for rare and longer for well done. Ask butcher about servings.

TIP: *The longer you cook a steak the drier it gets. If you are used to well-done steaks, try cooking them less each time you have them. You just might realize how good "medium" can be.*

Grilled Filet Mignon

4 (6 - 8 ounce) filets mignons
Seasoned salt
Cracked pepper

▶ After you start the charcoal or fire up the gas grill, season meat with seasoned salt and cracked black pepper and let meat reach room temperature.

▶ When charcoal has turned into red hot coals, put meat on grill. Cook for 3 to 5 minutes on each side according to taste. Serves 4.

TIP: *Thin steaks cook very fast. The best thickness for most steaks is about 2 inches. If meat is soft, it is rare. If it is firm, it is well-done.*

A Word About Steak

When you have an excellent cut like filet mignon, it isn't a good idea to cover up its natural flavor with sugary barbecue sauces. You would be well served to learn to appreciate natural flavors of all foods.

Pan-frying in butter sears the outside of the steak to hold in the juices. Start the steak on high heat just to sear the outside, then reduce heat. Do not overcook.

You will be brilliant when you learn how long to cook a steak for rare, medium rare, medium and well done. Remember what you did each time you cook a steak. These are expensive lessons.

Pork Main Dishes

Cherry Best Ham

1 (½ inch) thick center-cut ham slice
⅔ cup cherry preserves
½ teaspoon ground cinnamon
⅓ cup chopped walnuts

▶ Preheat oven to 325°.

▶ Place ham slice in 9 x 13-inch glass baking dish. Spread preserves over ham and sprinkle cinnamon over preserves. Top with chopped walnuts. Bake for 20 minutes. Serves 2 to 4.

Everyday Pork Roast or Beef Roast

Fresh ground peppercorns
1 (3 - 4 pound) pork or beef roast

▶ Preheat oven to 350°.

▶ Grind lots of peppercorns and sprinkle some salt all over roast.
Place in large roasting pan, add 1½ cups water and cook for
1 hour 30 minutes. Check occasionally to make sure there is
water in roasting pan. Cook longer if needed.

▶ Cool and slice across the grain. Serves 6 to 8.

TIP: Of course you can add additional seasonings like seasoned salt,
garlic powder, oregano and thyme. Play around with it.

Pork Roast Quesadillas

2 cups cooked, shredded pork roast
½ cup chunky salsa
2 teaspoons chili powder
¾ cup whole kernel corn
8 large whole wheat tortillas
1 (8 ounce) package shredded Mexican 4-cheese blend
1 (15 ounce) can pinto beans
Guacamole

▶ Combine pork roast, salsa, chili powder and corn in large bowl.
Spread mixture over 4 tortillas to within ½ inch of edge and
sprinkle cheese on top.

▶ Top with remaining tortillas and cook (1 at a time) in large non-
stick skillet on medium-high heat for about 5 minutes. Turn after
2 minutes or until light golden brown. Cut in wedges and serve
with pinto beans and guacamole. Serves 4 to 6.

TIP: This is another great reason to get into the habit of making a
roast. You get to make fantastic dishes with leftovers!

Ranch Pork Chops

6 (¾ inch) thick bone-in pork chops
Olive oil
2 (15 ounce) cans new potatoes, drained, quartered
1 onion, chopped
2 teaspoons garlic powder
¼ cup fresh chopped parsley
1 (8 ounce) carton sour cream
1 cup chicken or beef broth

▶ Place pork chops in oiled 6-quart oval slow cooker. Sprinkle pork chops with 1 teaspoon salt and ½ teaspoon pepper.

▶ Place potatoes around pork chops. Combine onion, garlic powder, parsley and sour cream in bowl and place around potatoes and chops. Pour broth over all. Cover and cook on LOW for 4 to 5 hours. Serves 4 to 6.

Parmesan-Covered Pork Chops

½ cup grated parmesan cheese
⅔ cup Italian seasoned breadcrumbs
1 egg
4 - 5 thin-cut pork chops
Olive oil

▶ Combine cheese and breadcrumbs in shallow bowl. Beat egg with 1 teaspoon water on shallow plate.

▶ Dip each pork chop in beaten egg then into breadcrumb mixture.

▶ Cook with a little oil in skillet over medium-high heat for about 5 minutes on each side or until golden brown. Serves 3 to 4.

Grilled Pork Chops

4 (1 inch) thick center-cut pork chops
2 - 3 tablespoons olive oil
1 lemon

▶ Start charcoal fire or gas grill. Allow pork chops to reach room temperature. When fire is ready, dry pork chops with paper towel and season with olive oil, a little lemon juice and a lot of salt and pepper.

▶ Place pork chops on very hot grill and sear both sides for 1 to 2 minutes to seal juices inside. Move to cooler part of grill and cook for 5 to 10 minutes or until chops are firm to touch and juices are clear.

▶ Remove chops from grill, drizzle with a little more lemon juice and serve immediately. Serves 4.

TIP: *Cooking time will vary with type of fire, thickness of chops and whether or not grill is covered. The main thing is not to overcook which dries out pork chops.*

Yee-Ha Pork Chops

1 (1 ounce) packet taco seasoning
4 (½ inch) thick boneless pork loin chops
1 tablespoon olive oil
Salsa

▶ Rub taco seasoning over pork chops. Brown pork chops in oil in skillet over medium heat.

▶ Add 2 tablespoons water, turn heat to low and simmer pork chops for about 30 to 40 minutes. (Check occasionally to see if water should be added.) Spoon salsa over pork chops to serve. Serves 4.

Pork Chop Supper

1 (18 ounce) package smoked pork chops
Butter
1 (12 ounce) jar pork gravy
¼ cup milk
1 (12 ounce) package very small new potatoes

▶ Brown pork chops in large skillet with butter. Pour gravy and milk into skillet and stir mixture around chops until they mix well.

▶ Add new potatoes around chops and gravy. Cover and simmer on medium heat for about 20 minutes. Serves 4.

TIP: *A healthier gravy for this recipe is miso gravy. Miso gravy is made by combining 3 tablespoons miso soup concentrate with 2 tablespoons arrowroot or kudzu root powder (cornstarch if you can't find the other options) and slowly mix in 1 cup water. Slowly bring the mix to a boil, stirring frequently until sauce thickens. Remove from heat.*

Tortellini-Tenderloin Supper

2 (9 ounce) packages fresh tortellini
1 (16 ounce) package frozen green peas, thawed
1 cup half-and-half cream
1 cup milk
¼ cup grated parmesan cheese
½ teaspoon garlic powder
2 - 3 cups cooked, cubed pork tenderloins or chops

▶ Cook tortellini according to package directions. Add green peas about 5 minutes before tortellini is done. Drain.

▶ Combine half-and-half cream, milk, parmesan, garlic powder and tenderloin pieces in saucepan; heat until thoroughly hot, but do not boil. Toss with tortellini and peas. Serve immediately. Serves 4 to 6.

Prizing-Winning Pork Tenderloin

This is a real treat. It's great as a leftover. The marinade is terrific and everyone will be impressed.

⅔ cup soy sauce
⅔ cup olive oil
2 tablespoons crystallized ginger, finely chopped
2 tablespoons real lime juice
1 teaspoon garlic powder
2 tablespoons minced onion
2 pork tenderloins

▶ Combine soy sauce, oil, ginger, lime juice, garlic powder and onion in bowl and pour over pork tenderloins. Marinate for about 36 hours.

▶ When ready to cook, drain and discard marinade. Cook on medium hot gas grill or charcoal fire for about 15 to 30 minutes. Don't overcook. Serves 8 to 10.

Grilled Pork Tenderloin with Rice

2 (1 pound) pork tenderloins
1 tablespoon olive oil
2 tablespoons jerk seasoning
1 cup cooked brown rice
1 (15 ounce) can black beans, rinsed
½ cup sliced roasted red bell pepper
2 tablespoons chopped cilantro

▶ Rub tenderloins with oil and sprinkle with jerk seasoning. Grill over medium-high heat for about 25 minutes and cook on both sides until juices run clear.

▶ Mix rice and beans and heat, add bell pepper, cilantro and a little salt and pepper. Spoon on serving platter. Slice tenderloin and arrange on top of rice-bean mixture. Serves 4 to 6.

TIP: Cooking rice is discussed on pages 179-181.

Hawaiian Aloha Pork

This is great served over rice.

1 (2 pound) package lean pork tenderloins, cut into 1-inch cubes
1 (15 ounce) can pineapple chunks with juice
1 (12 ounce) bottle chili sauce
1 teaspoon ground ginger

▶ Season pork with a little salt and pepper.

▶ Combine meat, pineapple with juice, chili sauce and ginger in skillet.

▶ Cover and simmer for 1 hour 30 minutes. Serves 4 to 6.

Italian Sausage and Ravioli

1 pound sweet Italian pork sausage, casing removed
1 (26 ounce) jar extra chunky mushroom and green
      pepper spaghetti sauce
2 cups chopped kale or fresh spinach
1 (24 ounce) package frozen cheese-filled ravioli, cooked, drained
Parmesan cheese

▶ Cook sausage according to package directions in large saucepan over medium heat or until brown and no longer pink and stir to separate meat. Stir in spaghetti sauce and kale. Heat through and add ravioli, stir occasionally.

▶ Pour into serving dish and sprinkle with parmesan cheese. Serves 4 to 6.

It is a fact that most people have a dozen or so meals that they eat for breakfast, lunch and dinner. They usually rotate these and introduce some minor variations throughout most of their lives. Choose your meals wisely.

Seafood Main Dishes

Baked Halibut

2 (1 inch) thick halibut steaks
1 (8 ounce) carton sour cream
½ cup grated parmesan cheese
¾ teaspoon dill weed
Paprika

▶ Preheat oven to 325°.

▶ Place halibut in sprayed 9 x 13-inch baking dish.

▶ Combine sour cream, parmesan cheese, dill weed and a little salt and pepper, if desired, in bowl. Spoon over halibut. Cover and bake for 20 minutes.

▶ Uncover and sprinkle with paprika. Bake for additional 10 minutes or until fish flakes easily with fork. Serves 2 to 3.

Delicious Grilled Fish

Everyone loves fried fish, but you'll be surprised to see how many raves you get with this easy grilling recipe.

8 - 10 catfish fillets
Garlic powder
Butter
Lemon

▶ Start charcoal or gas grill and heat to high temperature.

▶ Coat both sides of fillets with a little garlic powder, butter and lemon juice and place fish on sprayed or non-stick aluminum foil on grill.

▶ Cook for about 2 to 3 minutes on each side depending on heat from fire and thickness of fillets. Be careful not to overcook fish. It should not be dry. Serves 4 to 6.

Lemon-Baked Fish

1 pound sole or halibut fillets
2 tablespoons butter
1 teaspoon dried tarragon
2 tablespoons lemon juice

► Preheat oven to 375°.

► Place fish fillets in sprayed shallow pan with a little butter. Sprinkle with a little salt and pepper. Bake for 8 to 10 minutes.

► Turn and bake for additional 6 minutes or until fish flakes. Melt butter with tarragon and lemon juice. Serve over fish fillets. Serves 3 to 4.

Chipper Fish

2 pounds sole or orange roughy
½ cup Caesar salad dressing
1 cup crushed whole wheat crackers
¼ cup butter, melted
½ cup shredded cheddar cheese

► Preheat oven to 375°.

► Dip fish in dressing. Place in sprayed baking dish. Combine crackers, butter and cheese in bowl; sprinkle over fish. Bake for 25 minutes. Serves 4 to 6.

Crispy Flounder

⅓ cup mayonnaise
1 pound flounder fillets
1 cup seasoned breadcrumbs
¼ cup grated parmesan cheese

► Preheat oven to 375°.

► Place mayonnaise in small dish. Coat fish with mayonnaise and dip in crumbs to coat well.

► Arrange in shallow baking dish. Bake for 25 minutes. Before serving, sprinkle with parmesan. Serves 3 to 4.

Broiled Red Snapper

2 tablespoons dijon-style mustard
¼ cup Italian dressing
4 (6 ounce) red snapper fillets

► Preheat broiler.

► Combine mustard and Italian dressing in small bowl. Place snapper, skin-side down on sprayed foil-lined baking pan.

► Brush mustard-dressing mixture over fillets and broil for 8 minutes or until snapper flakes easily when tested with fork. Serves 4.

Skillet Shrimp Scampi

2 teaspoons olive oil
2 pounds shrimp, peeled, veined
⅔ cup herb-garlic marinade with lemon juice
¼ cup finely chopped green onions with tops
Rice, cooked

► Heat oil in large non-stick skillet. Add shrimp and marinade and cook, stirring often, until shrimp turns pink.

► Stir in green onions. Serve over rice. Serves 4 to 6.

Broiled Lemon-Garlic Shrimp

1 pound shrimp, peeled, veined
1 teaspoon garlic salt
2 tablespoons lemon juice
2 tablespoons butter

► Preheat broiler.

► Place shrimp in shallow baking pan. Sprinkle with garlic salt and lemon juice and dot with butter.

► Broil on one side for 3 minutes. Turn and broil for 3 minutes. Serves 4 to 6.

Sweet Things

Puddings
Fruit Desserts
Pies & Cobblers
Cookies & Bars

Leaving Home Cookbook
and Survival Guide

Sweet Things Contents

*All berries are super foods because they are absolutely
loaded with beneficial phytochemicals in the form
of antioxidants, flavonoids and beneficial acids.*

Puddings

Coconut-Rice Pudding

I am crazy about coconut because it has great health promoting qualities. This is a sweet dessert that is a perfect Healthy, Fast and Cheap™ companion to any meal.

2 cups cooked brown rice
½ (5.5 ounce) can coconut milk
2 tablespoons agave nectar
Ground cinnamon
½ teaspoon vanilla

▶ Mix rice, coconut milk and ½ cup water in pot. Bring to a light boil on medium heat, cover and reduce to simmer. Cook for 20 minutes and stir occasionally.

▶ Add agave nectar, cinnamon and vanilla to taste and cook for additional 5 minutes. Eat warm or let cool for a special treat. Serves 4 to 6.

TIP: *Additions include raisins, coconut flakes, dried cranberries or nuts, if desired.*

Creamy Banana Pudding

This is a quick and easy way to make the old favorite banana pudding.

1 (14 ounce) can sweetened condensed milk
1 (3.4 ounce) package instant vanilla pudding mix
1 (8 ounce) carton whipped topping, thawed
36 vanilla wafers
3 bananas

▶ Combine sweetened condensed milk and 1½ cups cold water in large bowl. Add pudding mix and beat well.

▶ Refrigerate for 5 minutes and fold in whipped topping.

▶ Slice bananas.

▶ Spoon 1 cup pudding mixture into 3-quart glass serving bowl. Top with one-third wafers, one-third bananas and one-third remaining pudding. Repeat layers twice and end with pudding. Cover and refrigerate. Serves 4 to 6.

Fruit Desserts

Chocolate-Covered Strawberries

These are very impressive and easy to make.

30 whole strawberries with stems
1 (12 ounce) package chocolate chips
6 tablespoons (¾ stick) butter

▶ Place clean dry berries with stems on large sheet of wax paper set on baking sheet.

▶ Melt chocolate chips in double boiler over hot water.

▶ Stir in butter and mix until it melts and blends well with chocolate.

▶ Dip very dry berries in chocolate, place on wax paper and refrigerate until chocolate is hard.

TIP: *If you do not have a double boiler, use a small saucepan for the chocolate and put it in a larger saucepan half filled with water.*

Kiwi Cream

Here's a great dessert with fresh fruit, a little brown sugar (or honey) and a splurge of chocolate syrup (or not). If you don't have a pear or kiwifruit, use whatever you've got. It will be great!

1 ripe pear
2 kiwifruit
1 cup seedless grapes
1 tablespoon brown sugar or honey
¼ cup plain milk yogurt
Chocolate syrup

▶ Peel and slice pear and kiwifruit and mix with grapes in 2 small bowls or dessert-type cups.

▶ In separate bowl, mix brown sugar and yogurt and pour over fruit. Drizzle chocolate syrup on top for a splurge. Serves 2.

Crazy Baked Apples

4 - 5 large baking apples
1 tablespoon lemon juice
⅓ cup Craisins®
½ cup chopped pecans
¼ cup honey
½ teaspoon ground cinnamon
¼ cup (½ stick) butter, softened
2 tablespoons each of butter and maple syrup, mixed
and warmed slightly

▶ Scoop out center of each apple and leave cavity about ½ inch from bottom. Peel top of apples down about 1 inch and brush lemon juice on peeled edges.

▶ Combine Craisins®, pecans, honey, cinnamon and butter in bowl. Spoon mixture into apple cavities.

▶ Pour ½ cup water in slow cooker and place apples on bottom.

▶ Cover and cook on LOW for 1 to 3 hours or until tender. Serve warm or at room temperature drizzled with warm maple syrup-butter mix. Serves 5.

Strawberry-Apple Crunch

¼ - ⅓ cup almond slivers
1 (10 ounce) package frozen unsweetened strawberries, thawed, peeled
2 cups chopped apples
2 (8 ounce) containers vanilla yogurt

▶ Spread almonds on baking pan and toast at 300° for about 5 to 7 minutes. Watch carefully so almonds don't burn. (This really brings out the flavors and is worth the effort.)

▶ Layer half strawberries, apples and yogurt in 3 parfait glasses or dessert-type cups. Repeat layers and top with toasted almonds. Serves 3.

Pies & Cobblers

Limeade Pie

1 (6 ounce) can frozen limeade concentrate, thawed
2 cups plain frozen yogurt, softened
1 (8 ounce) carton whipped topping, thawed
1 (6 ounce) ready graham cracker piecrust

▶ Combine limeade concentrate and yogurt in large bowl and mix well.

▶ Fold in whipped topping and pour into piecrust. Freeze for at least 4 hours or overnight. Serves 6 to 8.

Apple Crisp

5 cups peeled, cored, sliced apples
½ cup (1 stick) butter, melted
1 cup quick-cooking oats
½ cup firmly packed brown sugar
⅓ cup whole wheat flour

▶ Preheat over to 375°.

▶ Place apple slices in 8-inch or 9-inch square baking pan.

▶ Combine butter, oats, brown sugar and flour in bowl and sprinkle mixture over apples.

▶ Bake for 40 to 45 minutes or until apples are tender and topping is golden brown. Serves 4 to 5.

TIP: *As a variation, add 1 teaspoon ground cinnamon and ½ cup raisins or dried cranberries to apples before sprinkling with topping.*

Peach Cobbler

½ cup (1 stick) butter, melted
1 cup all-purpose flour or whole wheat flour
2¼ cups sugar, divided
2 teaspoons baking powder
1 cup milk
3 - 4 cups fresh, ripe sliced peaches
1 teaspoon ground cinnamon

▶ Preheat oven to 350°.

▶ Combine butter, flour, 1 cup sugar, baking powder and
¼ teaspoon salt in bowl, mix in milk and blend well.

▶ Spoon into sprayed 9 x 13-inch glass baking dish. Combine
sliced peaches, 1¼ cups sugar and cinnamon in bowl and pour
over dough.

▶ Bake for 1 hour. Crust will come to top. Serves 10 to 12.

Cookies & Bars

Easy Sugar Cookies

1 (8 ounce) package cream cheese, softened
¾ cup sugar
1 cup (2 sticks) butter
½ teaspoon lemon extract
2½ cups flour or whole wheat flour
Extra sugar

▶ Preheat oven to 375°.

▶ Combine cream cheese with sugar, butter and lemon extract in
medium bowl. Beat until ingredients blend well.

▶ Add flour and mix thoroughly.

▶ Drop round tablespoons of dough onto sprayed cookie sheet.

▶ Bake for 6 to 8 minutes.

▶ Remove from oven and immediately sprinkle sugar on each. Let
cookies cool for 1 minute on cookie sheet and transfer to cooling
rack or countertop. Yields 30 cookies.

Oatmeal Cookies

1 cup sugar
1 cup packed brown sugar
1 cup butter
2 eggs
2 teaspoons vanilla
1 teaspoon baking soda
1½ cups flour or whole wheat flour
3 cups old-fashioned oats
1 cup chopped pecans

▶ Preheat oven to 350°.

▶ Combine sugar, brown sugar, butter, eggs, 2 tablespoons water and vanilla in bowl and beat well.

▶ Add ½ teaspoon salt, baking soda and flour and mix. Add oats and pecans and mix.

▶ Drop tablespoonfuls of dough onto cookie sheet and bake for 14 to 15 minutes for crispy cookies, less for soft cookies. Yields 40 cookies.

Classic Peanut Butter Cookies

¾ cup (1½ sticks) butter, softened
1¼ cups crunchy peanut butter
1½ cups packed brown sugar or unrefined sugar
1 egg
1½ cups flour or whole grain flour
½ teaspoon baking powder
½ teaspoon baking soda

▶ Preheat oven to 350°.

▶ Cream butter, peanut butter, brown sugar and egg in large bowl and beat until creamy. Add remaining ingredients plus ½ teaspoon salt and mix.

▶ Use large cookie scoop to place cookies on cookie sheet. Make cookies thicker and larger than most cookies.

▶ Dip fork in water and flatten cookies slightly with criss-cross pattern. Bake for about 12 minutes. Yields 45 cookies.

Classic Toll House Chocolate Chip Cookies

The #1 cookie in America

2¼ cups flour
1 teaspoon baking soda
1 cup (2 sticks) butter, softened
¾ cup sugar
¾ cup packed brown sugar
1 teaspoon vanilla
2 eggs
1 (12 ounce) package semi-sweet chocolate chips
1 cup chopped pecans

▶ Preheat oven to 375°.

▶ Combine flour, baking soda and 1 teaspoon salt in medium bowl and set aside.

▶ In separate bowl, combine butter, sugar, brown sugar and vanilla and stir until creamy.

▶ Add eggs and mix thoroughly. Add flour mixture a little at a time and stir to mix well. Add chocolate chips and pecans and mix.

▶ Drop rounded tablespoonfuls of dough onto cookie sheet. Bake for about 8 minutes. Yields 30 cookies.

Molasses Cookies

½ cup coconut oil or ½ cup (1 stick) butter, softened
⅓ cup sugar
1 egg
½ cup dark molasses
¼ cup milk
½ cup wheat germ
1 cup whole wheat pastry flour
2 teaspoons baking powder
½ cup powdered milk

▶ Preheat oven to 325°.

▶ Mix oil, sugar, egg, molasses and milk in large bowl. In separate bowl, mix wheat germ, flour, baking powder and powdered milk.

▶ Add dry ingredients a little at a time to oil mixture and mix thoroughly.

▶ Drop spoonfuls of dough onto sprayed baking sheet.

▶ Bake for 10 to 12 minutes. Yields about 24 cookies.

Wheat Germ and Oatmeal Bars

This is a great alternative to energy bars!

¾ cup coconut oil
¾ cup honey
½ cup molasses
2 eggs
2 teaspoons vanilla
1 cup mixed raisins and nuts
1½ cups wheat germ
2 cups quick oats
¾ cup whole wheat pastry flour
½ cup whey protein powder or powdered milk

▶ Preheat oven to 350°.

▶ Mix all ingredients in bowl and spread mix into sprayed 9-inch square baking pan.

▶ Bake for 10 minutes.

▶ Cool and slice into bars. Refrigerate. Yields 9 bars.

Blueberry Sauce

1 (12 ounce) package frozen blueberries, thawed
⅓ cup sugar
¼ cup lime juice
1½ teaspoons cornstarch

▶ Simmer blueberries, sugar and lime juice in saucepan until they are soft and mash together.

▶ Mix cornstarch with ¼ cup water in bowl to make paste.

▶ Slowly mix paste into simmering berries and simmer until sauce thickens.

TIP: *Serve over ice cream, biscuits, pound cake or yogurt. Any berry is good in this recipe.*

Basic Pound Cake

1½ cups (3 sticks) butter
3 cups sugar
8 eggs
3 cups flour

▶ Preheat oven to 300°.

▶ Cream butter and sugar in bowl and mix well.

▶ Add eggs one at a time, beating well after each addition. Add flour in small amounts at a time.

▶ Pour into sprayed, floured 10-inch bundt pan and bake for 1 hour 30 minutes. Do not open oven door during baking. Serves 18.

Goji berries are about the size of raisins and taste like a cross between cherries and cranberries. They have the highest antioxidant power of any fruit. Sprinkle them on your cereal, oatmeal or in your yogurt or eat them as a snack.

Glossary of Terms

Adobo

A seasoning available from Goya Foods. My wife is Puerto Rican and uses this all the time. It is available in the Latin food section of the store.

Bragg Liquid Aminos

A version of soy sauce made exclusively from soybeans. This is an option for people that are avoiding fermented foods. Available at health food stores or the natural foods section of your local grocery store.

Coconut Oil

This oil is pressed from mature coconut meat. Look for "Extra Virgin" coconut oil pressed without high heat or chemical solvents. It is a stable oil, which prevents rancidity and it is 97% saturated. Most of the bad press on saturated fats should be directed towards low quality animal fats and hydrogenated "trans fats".

Coconut Milk

This is a rich, creamy milk made by grinding up coconut meat, cooking it with water and then squeezing out the liquid from the mash.

Coconut Water

This is the liquid that is naturally occurring in young coconuts. This should not be confused with coconut milk. Coconut water has an electrolyte profile similar to human blood plasma. It is the most hydrating drink for humans next to water.

Earth Balance® Spreads

Non-hydrogenated butter-like spreads.

Gomasio

A sesame seed salt.

Glycemic Index

This is a scale for rating the speed at which foods turn into glucose in your body. Though helpful, it is not a stand alone determinant of the overall health and appropriateness of your food.

Glycemic Load

This is the glycemic index multiplied by the caloric density of each food. This index is a much better indicator of the health or harm spectrum that a food lands on.

Goji Berry

Also knows as Chinese wolfberry, lycium fruit and gouqi, this little fruit packs a punch. Goji is a colloquial term for a particular strain of wolfberry, but most strains are referred to as goji today. The goji berry offers tons of antioxidants, free radical scavengers, and a full profile of essential amino and fatty acids. This is an amazing high-energy food.

Green Drink

Any powdered food supplement that features chlorophyll-rich foods such as wheat grass, barley grass, chlorella, spirulina, etc.

Honey

There are three forms that I especially want to mention.

Unheated honey is one of my favorite foods on the planet. Unheated honey retains all enzymes. It is the most enzyme active food on the planet. Enzyme rich foods assist in digestion and assimilation of anything else you eat.

Raw honey is honey that has been heated to 160° for processing. It retains some of the enzyme activity but tends to lose a great deal of other micronutrients like propolis and pollen. Pollen is a great source of flavonoids (beneficial plant compounds). Propolis is known to be stimulating to the immune system.

Pasteurized honey is basically the same as sucrose. I would not recommend it.

Hydrogenated Oil

Made from the cheapest oil producing plants possible, usually cottonseed, corn and soybeans. Oil is extracted through a high heat press (which quickly promotes rancidity) then additionally extracted with hexane. The hexane is removed and other "impurities" (vitamins, minerals, essential fatty acids) are removed to ensure a predictable end product. The oil is then whipped in a vacuum centrifuge with the addition of a metal catalyst, usually nickel shavings and hydrogen molecules. New molecular structures are formed which are referred to as "trans" fatty acids. Walter Willet, principle member of the Harvard-based Nurses' Health Study (the largest single controlled study in human history) suggests that hydrogenated oil is the worst food that we are currently consuming. (Corn syrup is a close second.)

Macronutrients

Carbohydrates, protein and fat.

Micronutrients

Vitamins, minerals, essential fatty acids, amino acids, phytochemicals, enzymes.

Miso

A cultured bean paste traditionally made from soybeans, it's also available made from chick-peas, barley and rice. It's a great source of beneficial enzymes and protein with a savory rich flavor.

Mung Beans

A small green bean that cooks like a lentil. They are easy to digest, quick to cook and high in protein.

Nutritional Yeast

A tasty flake or powder that can be added to soups, sandwiches, popcorn, rice, veggies or toast. It has a nutty flavor and is super high in protein and B-vitamins.

Olive Oil

Get extra virgin olive oil in opaque glass or in metal containers.

Protein Powder

Any concentrated protein supplement added to smoothies, cereals or other foods and beverages.

Soy Protein or Soy Protein Isolate: A refined food that may be hard for many people to digest and assimilate. (Not my first choice.)

Rice Protein: A good choice for those wishing to increase protein in the diet with less digestive disturbance. Good for people with soy sensitivities or allergies who also choose a vegetarian diet.

Whey protein is made from the by-products of the cheese-making industry. This food is free of lactose and casein which often trigger food sensitivities.

Raw Cacao

This is the stuff all chocolate is made from. The raw form is the nut from the cacao tree fermented in the fruit pulp of the plant for a few days and sun- or air-dried. It is an amazingly nutritious food with healthy fats, tons of magnesium and selenium, and more chemical complexity than any other food on the planet.

Sesame Tahini

A refined sesame seed paste. Look for whole sesame seed paste, whole sesame seed butter or for tahini that is made from whole sesame seeds.

Soba Noodles

Traditional Japanese noodles made from buckwheat, often with whole wheat and yam in the ingredients.

Sprouted Grains

Sprouted grains are easier to digest, more nutritious and maintain freshness. Sprouted grain bread should be purchased from the freezer or refrigerator section.

Tamari

A salty, earthy condiment made from soybeans. A lot of supermarket soy sauce is made from isolated soy protein and caramel color and is not a healthy choice. Look for a good quality fermented soy sauce like Eden® Foods brand.

Whey

The liquid from cultured dairy. The simplest way to have whey on hand for use when soaking grains is to make yogurt cheese. Whey is a lactic acid starter that assists in predigesting the grains as well.

Recommended Reading

Beaman, Andrea. *The Whole Truth: Eating & Recipe Guide* pub. Andrea Beaman, HHC 2006 ISBN: 0977869318

Becker, Gretchen. *Prediabetes: What you need to know to keep diabetes away*, Marlow & Co., 2005 ISBN: 1569244642

Cherniske, Stephen. *Caffeine Blues*, Warner Books, 1998 ISBN: 0446673919

David, Marc. *Nourishing Wisdom*, Harmony/Bell Tower 1994 ISBN: 0517881292

Diamond, John. *Life Energy*, Continuum International Publishing Group, 1990 ISBN: 1557782814

Douillard, John. *The 3-Season Diet*, Three Rivers Press, 2001 ISBN: 0609805436

Dufty, William. *Sugar Blues*, Warner Books, 1986 ISBN: 0446343129

Erasmus, Udo, PhD. *Fats That Heal, Fats That Kill*, Alive Books, 1993 ISBN: 0920470386

Fallon, Sally & Enig, Mary. *Nourishing Traditions: The Cookbook That Challenges Politically Correct Nutrition and the Diet Dictocrats*, New Trends Publishing, Inc. 1999 ISBN: 0967089735

Gittleman, Ann-Louise. *Get the Sugar Out: 501 Simple Ways to Cut the Sugar Out of Any Diet*, Three Rivers Press, 1996 ISBN: 0517886537

Lipski, Elizabeth, PhD. *Digestive Wellness*, McGraw-Hill, 2004 ISBN: 0071441964

Lyman, Howard. *Mad Cowboy: Plain Truth from the Cattle Rancher Who Won't Eat Meat*, Scribner 2001 ISBN: 0684854465

Maurer, Robert, PhD. *One Small Step Can Change Your Life: The Kaizen Way*, Workman Publishing Group, 2004 ISBN: 0761129235

Nestle, Marion, PhD. *Food Politics: How the Food Industry Influences Nutrition and Health*, University of California Press, 2003 ISBN: 0520240677

Nestle, Marion, PhD. *What to Eat*, North Point Press, 2006 ISBN: 0865477043

Pitchford, Paul. *Healing with Whole Foods*, North Atlantic Books, 2002 ISBN: 1556434308

Pollan, Michael. *The Omnivore's Dilemma: A Natural History of Four Meals*, Penguin Press, 2006 ISBN: 1594200823

Rosedale, Ron. *The Rosedale Diet*, Collins, 2005 ISBN: 006056573X

Rosenthal, Joshua, M. Ed. *Integrative Nutrition: the Future of Nutrition*, Integrative Nutrition Publishing, 2006 ISBN: 0977302504

Roth, Geneen. *Breaking Free from Emotional Eating*, Plume Books, New York, 2003 ISBN: 0452284910

Roth, Geneen. *When Food Is Love*, Plume Books, New York, 1992 ISBN: 0452268184

Schlosser, Eric. *Fast Food Nation: The Dark Side of the All-American Meal*, Harper Perennial, 2002 ISBN: 0060938455

Willett, Walter, M.D. *Eat, Drink and Be Healthy*, Free Press, 2005 ISBN: 0743266420

Wolfe, David. *The Sunfood Diet Success System*, Maul Bros. Publishing, 2000 ISBN: 0965353338

Index

Cookbooks Published by Cookbook Resources, LLC
Bringing Family and Friends to the Table

*The Best of Cooking
with 3 Ingredients*

*The Ultimate Cooking
with 4 Ingredients*

Easy Cooking with 5 Ingredients

Healthy Cooking with 4 Ingredients

*Gourmet Cooking
with 5 Ingredients*

*4-Ingredient Recipes
for 30-Minute Meals*

Essential 3-4-5 Ingredient Recipes

The Best 1001 Short, Easy Recipes

1001 Fast Easy Recipes

1001 Community Recipes

*Busy Woman's
Quick & Easy Recipes*

*Busy Woman's
Slow Cooker Recipes*

Easy Slow Cooker Cookbook

Easy One-Dish Meals

Easy Potluck Recipes

Easy Casseroles

Easy Desserts

Sunday Night Suppers

Easy Church Suppers

365 Easy Meals

365 Easy Soups and Stews

365 Easy Vegetarian Recipes

365 Easy Chicken Recipes

365 Easy One-Dish Recipes

365 Easy Pasta Recipes

365 Easy Slow Cooker Recipes

365 Easy Soup Recipes

Quick Fixes with Cake Mixes

*Kitchen Keepsakes/
More Kitchen Keepsakes*

Gifts for the Cookie Jar

All New Gifts for the Cookie Jar

Muffins In A Jar

The Big Bake Sale Cookbook

*Classic Tex-Mex
and Texas Cooking*

Classic Southwest Cooking

Miss Sadie's Southern Cooking

Texas Longhorn Cookbook

Cookbook 25 Years

A Little Taste of Texas

A Little Taste of Texas II

*Trophy Hunters'
Wild Game Cookbook*

Recipe Keeper

*Leaving Home Cookbook
and Survival Guide*

*Classic Pennsylvania
Dutch Cooking*

Easy Diabetic Recipes

cookbook resources LLC

www. cookbookresources.com
Your Ultimate Source for Easy Cookbooks

How to Order: **Leaving Home Cookbook and Survival Guide**
Order online at www.cookbookresources.com

Or Call Toll Free: (866) 229-2665   Or Mail to: Cookbook Resources
         Fax: (972) 317-6404   541 Doubletree Drive
                                              Highland Village, Texas 75077

Please send ____ copies @ $16.95 (U.S.) each $ _____

Texas residents add sales tax @ $1.40 each $ _____

Plus postage/handling @ $6.00 (1ˢᵗ copy) $ _____

Plus postage/handling @ $1.00 per each additional copy $ _____

Check or Credit Card (Canada – credit card only) Total $ _____

Charge to: ☐ MasterCard ☐ VISA   Expiration Date ⌞_⌟ ⌞_⌟ (mm/yy)

Account No. ⌞__⌟ ⌞__⌟ ⌞__⌟ ⌞__⌟

Signature _____

Name (please print) _____

Address _____

City _____ State/Prov. _____ Zip/Postal Code _____

Telephone (Day) _____ (Evening) _____

- -

How to Order: **Leaving Home Cookbook and Survival Guide**
Order online at www.cookbookresources.com

Or Call Toll Free: (866) 229-2665   Or Mail to: Cookbook Resources
         Fax: (972) 317-6404   541 Doubletree Drive
                                              Highland Village, Texas 75077

Please send ____ copies @ $16.95 (U.S.) each $ _____

Texas residents add sales tax @ $1.40 each $ _____

Plus postage/handling @ $6.00 (1ˢᵗ copy) $ _____

Plus postage/handling @ $1.00 per each additional copy $ _____

Check or Credit Card (Canada – credit card only) Total $ _____

Charge to: ☐ MasterCard ☐ VISA   Expiration Date ⌞_⌟ ⌞_⌟ (mm/yy)

Account No. ⌞__⌟ ⌞__⌟ ⌞__⌟ ⌞__⌟

Signature _____

Name (please print) _____

Address _____

City _____ State/Prov. _____ Zip/Postal Code _____

Telephone (Day) _____ (Evening) _____

Leaving Home
COOKBOOK
and Survival Guide

*The How-to's of Eating
Healthy, Fast and Cheap*™

cookbook
resources® LLC

www.cookbookresources.com